The Charge Description Master Handbook

Anne B. Casto,
RHIA, CCS

ISBN: 978-1-58426-250-3
AHIMA Product No.: AB101010

AHIMA Staff:
Claire Blondeau, MBA, Senior Editor
Cynthia Douglas Chernoff, Developmental Editor
Katie Greenock, Editorial and Production Coordinator
Ashley Sullivan, Assistant Editor
Ken Zielske, Director of Publications
Judy Bielby, MBA, RHIA, CCS, CPHQ, External Content Reviewer

All information contained within this book, including Web sites and regulatory information, was current and valid as of the date of publication. However, Web page addresses and the information on them may change or disappear at any time and for any number of reasons. The user is encouraged to perform his or her own general Web searches to locate any site addresses listed here that are no longer valid.

This publication is designed to provide accurate and authoritative information in regard to the subject matter covered. It is sold with the understanding that the publisher is not engaged in rendering legal, accounting, or other professional services. If legal advice or other expert assistance is required, the services of a competent professional person should be sought.

All products mentioned in this book are either trademarks of the companies referenced in this book, registered trademarks of the companies referenced in this book, or neither.

American Health Information Management Association
233 North Michigan Avenue, 21st Floor
Chicago, Illinois 60601-5809

ahima.org

Contents

About the Author and Contributors

Anne B. Casto, RHIA, CCS, is the President of Casto Consulting, LLC. Casto Consulting, LLC is a consulting firm that provides services to hospitals and other healthcare stakeholders primarily in the areas of reimbursement and coding. Casto Consulting, LLC specializes in linking coding and billing practices to positive revenue cycle outcomes. Additionally, the firm provides guidance to consulting firms, healthcare organizations and healthcare insurers regarding reimbursement methodologies and Medicare regulations.

Prior to founding the firm, Anne was the Program Manager of the HIMS Division at The Ohio State University School of Allied Medical Professions. Ms. Casto taught healthcare reimbursement, ICD-9-CM coding and CPT coding courses for several years. Additionally, Ms. Casto was responsible for curriculum revisions in the areas of Chargemaster management, clinical data management and healthcare reimbursement.

Additionally, Ms. Casto was the Vice President of Clinical Information for Cleverley & Associates, where she worked very closely with APC regulations and guidelines, preparing hospitals for the implementation of the Medicare OPPS. Ms. Casto was also the Clinical Information Product Manager for CHIPS/Ingenix. She joined CHIPS/Ingenix in 1998 and spent the majority of her time developing coding compliance products for the inpatient and outpatient settings.

Ms. Casto has been responsible for inpatient and outpatient coding activities in several large hospitals including Mt. Sinai Medical Center (NYC), Beth Israel Medical Center (NYC), and The Ohio State University. She has worked extensively with CMI, quality measures, physician documentation, and coding accuracy efforts at these facilities.

Ms. Casto received her degree in Health Information Management at The Ohio State University in 1995. She received her Certified Coding Specialist credential in 1998 from the American Health Information Management Association. Ms. Casto recently coauthored an AHIMA-published text book entitled *Principles of Healthcare Reimbursement.* Additionally, Ms. Casto was a contributing author to the recently published AHIMA books: *Severity DRGs and Reimbursement, An MS-DRG Primer* and *Effective Management of Coding Services.* Ms. Casto received the AHIMA Legacy Award in 2007, part of the FORE Triumph Awards, which honors a significant contribution to the knowledge base of the HIM field through an insightful publication. Additionally, Ms. Casto was honored with the Ohio Health Information Management Association's Distinguished Member Award in 2008.

Erica Leeds, MS, RHIA, CCS, CCS-P, is the project coordinator for Revenue Cycle Solutions at Clarian Health Partners in Indianapolis, Indiana. Her previous roles included Chargemaster coordinator, coding manager, Chargemaster consultant, clinical auditor, and adjunct lecturer for the Health Information Administration Program in Indianapolis, Indiana. She has been actively involved with Indiana Health Information Management Association (IHIMA), where she has held many leadership positions, including Past President. She is also a past president of the Central Indiana HIMA. She has given numerous presentations at regional, state, and national conferences. She has been a contributing author for *Effective Management of Coding Services* for the last three editions.

Margery Mazoh, MS, is the Director of Chargemaster and Pricing Services at the Cleveland Clinic, where she has worked since 2001 in positions including Senior Project Manager and Revenue Cycle Manager in Fiscal Services, among others. She has more than 20 years' experience in healthcare management, administration, strategy, and analytics. She earned her Master of Science in Health Policy and Management from the Harvard School of Public Health and her bachelor's degree in sociology from Haverford College. She has been published in *hfm*, the journal of the Healthcare Financial Management Association, and has made numerous presentations on the topics of value-based pricing strategy and implementation planning.

John Richey, MBA, RHIA, is the founding Program Director and Instructor of Health Informatics at the University of Findlay in Findlay, Ohio. Richey also founded the Health Information Technology program at Terra Community College in Fremont, Ohio, where he served as Program Director and Assistant Professor. Previous positions include Administrative Director/Manager, Occupational Health Services at Mercy Hospital of Tiffin, in Tiffin, Ohio; Regional Manager–Chargemaster and Senior Financial Analyst–Decision Support at Mercy Health Partners, in Toledo, Ohio; Director of Medical Records/Registration at Mercy Hospital of Tiffin; and Director of Medical Records at Bucyrus Community Hospital in Bucyrus, Ohio. He has written for *Journal of the American Health Information Management Association*. He has served on the AHIMA Nominating Committee and is a past chair of the Delegate Workgroup. Richey is a past president of the Ohio Health Information Management Association (OHIMA) and served on the board for many years. Professional honors include AHIMA Best Practice Award–Lotus Notes Chargemaster Management, and the OHIMA Distinguished Member Award. Richey earned his Master of Business Administration from Tiffin University and his Bachelor of Science in Allied Health Professions from The Ohio State University.

Susan White, PhD, CHDA, is a Clinical Associate Professor in the HIM Department at The Ohio State University. She teaches classes in statistics, data analytics, healthcare finance and computer applications. Prior to joining OSU, Dr. White was the Vice

President of Research and Development for Cleverley + Associates and the Vice President of Data Operations for CHIPS/Ingenix.

Dr. White has written numerous books and articles regarding the benchmarking of healthcare facilities and the appropriate use of claims data. She has published articles in the areas of outcomes assessment and risk adjustment using healthcare financial and clinical data. Dr. White has presented to national audiences on the topics of heath care data analysis, hospital benchmarking and claims data mining.

Dr. White received her PhD in Statistics from The Ohio State University in 1991.

Preface

The Charge Description Master (CDM) has been a component of the healthcare facility revenue cycle for many years. However, the role of the CDM has drastically changed over the past ten years with the implementation of the Center for Medicare and Medicaid Services (CMS) Outpatient Prospective Payment System (OPPS). A table that once held hospital prices is now a dynamic database that houses not only prices but critical claim data elements. Maintenance and management of the CDM has in turn become a full-time position at most facilities, often with a staff or team dedicated to producing complete and compliant CDM data that is vital to the production of complete and accurate healthcare claims. *The Charge Description Master Handbook* was created to be a reference manual for CDM coordinators and managers. The information provided in this text will provide coordinators and mangers not only with CDM basics but also with best practices, problem solving skills, and a solid understanding of CDM compliance necessities.

About the Terminology Used in *The Charge Description Master Handbook*

Each CDM is designed and customized to meet the needs of the facility. Therefore, terminology used in and around the CDM varies from facility to facility. In this text the authors came to consensus and used the terminology that they believed was most common in the CDM community. However, that is not to say that different terminology used at your facility is inaccurate or out of date. For example, in this text the term *charge code* is used to describe the facility-specific number assigned to line items in the CDM. Not all facilities use the term *charge code*. Other terminology, such as *service code*, *item code*, *charge item code*, and *charge identifier code,* is also used throughout the CDM community. The authors chose a standard terminology set for this text in order to keep the information consistent and so that the reader would not become confused or disoriented by varying terms when moving from chapter to chapter.

The Charge Description Master Handbook Structure

The CDM Handbook was created to provide CDM analysts, managers, and coordinators with the foundation necessary to be successful in the maintenance and management of the CDM at their facility. Each chapter discusses a different component of CDM management. As managers and coordinators move through this text, they will acquire the knowledge necessary to develop and manage CDM processes and procedures at their facility.

Chapter 1, Charge Description Master, provides a history of the CDM as well as current perspectives on the utilization of the CDM in the healthcare revenue cycle. As the reader begins to understand the evolution of the CDM, he or she can begin to understand why such a strong emphasis has been placed on the maintenance and management of the CDM over the past few years.

Chapter 2, Charge Description Master Structure, provides a detailed look at which data elements are included in a typical CDM. For each data element, key information has been provided to assist CDM managers with following best practices to develop and maintain the CDM at their facility.

Chapter 3, Charge Description Master Maintenance, provides an in-depth look at the maintenance process. Basic components of a maintenance plan are provided in order to assist managers and coordinators with developing their own plans.

Chapter 4, Managing CDM Workflow, gives a step-by-step look at developing and executing CDM workflows. This in-depth examination at this crucial area of CDM management will help managers and coordinators analyze and modify workflows at their facilities.

Chapter 5, The Relationship between Charge Description Master and Compliance, provides a detailed discussion surrounding compliance guidance and the process of ensuring compliance at your facility. The coding and billing process is a highly regulated process. Therefore, this chapter was designed to assist managers and coordinators with understanding the where, when, why, and how of CDM compliance.

Chapter 6, Corporate Charge Description Masters, provides the reader with an in-depth look at CDM standardization, also known as CDM consolidation. If your facility is part of a hospital system, then this chapter is a must-read. The chapter provides case studies that illustrate best practices in CDM standardization.

Chapter 7, Charge Description Master Audits, discusses the audit process from beginning to end. Best practices, key audit elements and pitfalls are discussed in detail. This chapter provides the reader with a step-by-step look at creating and executing a CDM audit.

Chapter 8, Pricing, provides an overview of how prices (charges, rate, and so on) are established. Though the CDM coordinator or manager may not be responsible for pricing, it is important for the CDM team members to understand how prices are set at their facility. A thorough discussion on the importance of price transparency is also provided in this chapter.

Chapter 9, Managing High-Risk Areas, provides a look at some typically troublesome CDM areas. This look at advanced CDM issues will provides the reader with helpful suggestions and ways to problem solve within high-risk areas before a compliance issue arises.

Acknowledgments

The authors wish to thank Judy Bielby, MBA, RHIA, CCS, CPHQ, who served as external reviewer for the text.

In addition, they wish to thank their families for their never-ending support.

Chapter 1

Charge Description Master (CDM)

Anne B. Casto, RHIA, CCS

What is the Charge Description Master? It has many different names in the healthcare community: Chargemaster, price compendium, service master. The most common name is the Charge Description Master or CDM. The CDM is essentially a database that houses required claim components associated with inpatient and outpatient services rendered to patients during the delivery of healthcare services. You may wonder why this specific database requires its own text. In today's healthcare environment, the CDM is crucial to the production of a complete and accurate hospital claim. A complete and accurate claim is essential to the reimbursement health of a hospital. And without reimbursement for services performed, hospitals would not be able to provide care for patients, expand technologies, and engage in critical healthcare research. The CDM is a critical component of a hospital's financial health.

Historical Perspectives

Prior to the implementation of the Outpatient Prospective Payment System (OPPS) by the Centers for Medicare and Medicaid Services (CMS) in 2000 (Casto and Layman 2010) for use in the Medicare hospital outpatient setting, the CDM was primarily used to house the charge or price for hospital services. Since a retrospective cost-based system was used by CMS prior to 2000, only the revenue code and charge were required to complete the reimbursement formula. Therefore, not much attention was paid to the CDM except for the maintenance of the charge or price.

However, a whole new outlook for the CDM came with the implementation of OPPS. Reimbursement changed from a retrospective cost-based payment system to a prospective procedure-based payment system. The Current Procedural Terminology (CPT) and HCPCS Level II codes became very important data elements that determined the reimbursement level rather than simply the charge reported by the facility.

With procedure-based payment came a whole new set of billing and coding requirements. Revised and new regulations were introduced to the hospital community. Suddenly there were rules surrounding which CPT codes could be reported with certain revenue codes, which revenue codes required that a CPT code be reported, which modifiers should be reported and when, and the like. With the regulations came new fraud and abuse issues. The regulations surrounding billing and coding compliance will be discussed in detail in chapter 5 of this text.

Additionally, over the past several years there has been a call for increased healthcare transparency. Healthcare transparency is a movement where consumers of healthcare are provided with information about the quality and cost of healthcare services so that they can choose healthcare providers based on value. It is a two-part equation: consumers not only need to understand and have access to quality and outcomes reports, but they also need to be able to compare those figures with cost or price data from the corresponding facilities. The thought is that consumers will then gravitate toward providers that are able to render high quality care at an affordable price, giving the healthcare consumers good value for their healthcare dollars. Though healthcare transparency is in the beginning stages of popularity in the United States, many states, including California, have passed laws requiring hospitals to publish their charges or prices to the public to help promote the healthcare transparency movement. Healthcare transparency will be discussed in detail in chapter 8 of this text.

With this new outlook of the CDM came new uses and new perspectives regarding the management of the CDM. Over the past several years the evolution of the CDM has been tremendous. CDM Coordinator positions have become highly sought after positions in the Finance department. Key performance indicators have been established for the CDM unit. Coding and claiming compliance is at the forefront of hospitals' agendas.

Hospital Revenue Cycle

Note: This section was adapted from Casto and Layman 2010.

To fully appreciate the role of the CDM, one must first understand the revenue cycle at a healthcare facility. The revenue cycle is a regular recurring cycle of activities that results in the payment of services provided by a healthcare facility. Revenue cycle management is the management of that recurring cycle. Although the complexity of the revenue cycle depends upon the strategy and size of the facility, there are four main components of a revenue cycle. Figure 1.1 shows the four major revenue cycle components.

Revenue Cycle Components

Have you ever wondered how a hospital claim is produced? We are all familiar with how retail bills are produced, for example at the grocery store or department store; they are pretty straightforward. You take the items you want to purchase to

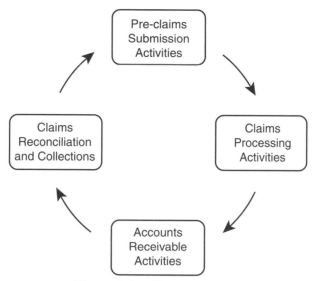

Figure 1.1.   Revenue cycle

the checkout, the items are entered into the cash register, a bill is produced, and the consumer pays the bill on site with cash or credit. It is much more complicated at a healthcare facility. For example, purchasers of healthcare often need to be pre-approved for purchase. Third-party-payer contracts require different data elements for the bill. Reimbursement rates vary from payer to payer. It indeed can be very complicated. We will discuss the four main components of the revenue cycle to explore just how a hospital bill is produced and then managed throughout the reimbursement process.

Pre-claims Submission Activities

Pre-claims submission activities consist of tasks and functions from the admitting and case-management areas. Specifically, this portion of the revenue cycle is responsible for collecting the patient's and responsible parties' information completely and accurately for determining the appropriate financial class. Additionally, in this step of the revenue cycle, the patient is educated as to his or her ultimate financial responsibility for services rendered, collecting waivers when appropriate, and verifying data prior to procedures or services being performed and submitted for payment. For example, when a Medicare patient arrives for admission into the cardiology unit for a coronary artery stent placement, the admitting representative is responsible for collecting the patient's demographic data including the individual's Medicare health insurance claim number (HICN) (CMS 2008). Additionally, the Medicare patient may need to be educated about any annual deductible amount or copayment responsibilities if the inpatient stay were to last longer than 60 days (CMS 2008).

Claims Processing Activities

Claims processing activities include the capture of all billable services, claim generation, and claim corrections. Charge capture is a vital component of the revenue cycle. All clinical areas that provide services to a patient must report charges for the services that they have performed. Failure to report charges for these services will result in lost reimbursement for the healthcare facility. Charge capture can be accomplished in a variety of ways depending on the technological capabilities of the healthcare facility.

Order Entry

Electronic order entry systems have been implemented at hospitals to help capture the charge at the point of service delivery. With an electronic order entry system, the charge for the service or supply is automatically transferred to the patient accounting system and posted to the patient's claim. Facilities without electronic systems use paper-based processes such as charge tickets, superbills, or encounter forms to assist in charge collection. With a paper-based process, the paper forms are collected and then entered into the patient accounting system, where the charge is then transferred to the claim. The paper system leaves more room for error because charges can be posted to the wrong patient's account, digits can be transposed during data entry, and backlogs can occur when data entry clerks are absent or pulled off task.

Coding is a major component of charge capture. Claims submission regulations require ICD-9-CM or HCPCS Level I and II codes reported on a patient's claim depending on whether the visit is inpatient or outpatient (HHS 2003, 8381). And, as previously discussed, for many payers including Medicare, the HCPCS code determines the level of reimbursement for hospital outpatient claims. There are two ways in which HCPCS codes are transferred to the bill.

Charge Description Master

Several types of visits, such as clinic visits, or services such as laboratory or radiology, are designed to have procedure codes posted to the claim via the CDM. During order entry, whether electronic or paper-based, a unique charge identifier for each service is entered. This unique identifier triggers a charge from the CDM to be posted to the patient's account. When part of the charge is the HCPCS code, then the coding process is known as hard coding.

Coding by Health Information Management (HIM)

Other types of visits, such as inpatient or complex ambulatory surgery, require the diagnoses and operating room procedures to be coded by health information management (HIM) professionals. During the coding process, medical records are reviewed by the coding staff. All diagnoses and procedures are identified, coded, and then abstracted into the HIM coding system. This system then transfers the diagnoses and procedure codes to the patient accounting system where they are posted to the patient's claim prior to submission for payment. This coding process is known as soft coding or HIM coding.

Auditing and Review

Once all data have been posted to a patient's account, the claim can be reviewed for accuracy and completeness. Many facilities have internal auditing systems known as scrubbers. The auditing system runs each claim through a set of edits specifically designed for that third-party payer. The auditing system identifies data that have failed edits and flags the claim for correction. Examples of errors that cause claim rejections or denials if not caught by the scrubber are:

- Incompatible dates of service
- Nonspecific or inaccurate diagnosis and procedure codes
- Lack of medical necessity
- Inaccurate revenue code assignment

The auditing process prevents facilities from sending incomplete or inaccurate claims to the payer. Facilities that do not have an editing system may perform a hand audit of a sample of claims. HIM and reimbursement specialists review claims with the medical record to determine if all services, diagnoses, and procedures were accurately reported. If errors are found, they can be corrected before claim submission.

Once reviewed and corrected, the claim can be submitted to the third-party payer for payment. The Health Insurance Portability and Accountability Act of 1996 (HIPAA) added a new part to the Social Security Act titled Administrative Simplification. The purpose of this section is to improve the efficiency and effectiveness of the healthcare delivery system. Through this section, standards and requirements for the electronic exchange of certain health information were established (HHS 2003, 8381). The Final Rule on Standards for Electronic Transactions and Code Sets, also known as the Transactions Rule, identified eight electronic transactions and six code sets (see tables 1.1 and 1.2). This Rule requires that all providers, third-party payers, claims clearinghouses, and so forth use the same sets of codes to communicate coded health information; therefore requiring standardization for systems and applications across the healthcare continuum (HHS 2003, 8381). Not only does this support standardization, but it also supports administrative simplification. Providers can now maintain a select number of code sets at their current version, rather than maintaining different versions (current and old) of many code sets based on payer specification as required in the past.

Healthcare claims, healthcare payment and remittance advice, and coordination of benefits are included in the electronic transactions. As of October 16, 2003, with the exception of those from small providers and under certain limited circumstances, all healthcare

Table 1.1. HIPAA electronic transactions

Healthcare claims or equivalent encounter information
Eligibility for a health plan
Referral certification and authorization
Healthcare claim status
Enrollment and disenrollment in a health plan
Healthcare payment and remittance advice
Health plan premium payments
Coordination of benefits

Source: HHS 2003, 8383.

Table 1.2. HIPAA code sets

International Classification of Diseases, 9th Edition, Clinical Modification, Volumes 1 and 2
International Classification of Diseases, 9th Edition, Clinical Modification, Volume 3
National Drug Codes
Code on Dental Procedures and Nomenclature
Health Care Financing Administration Common Procedure Coding System
Current Procedural Terminology, 4th Edition

Source: HHS 2003, 8382.

facilities were required to electronically submit and receive Medicare healthcare claims, remittance advices, and coordination of benefits (CMS 2003). Generally speaking, facilities submit claims via the 837I electronic format, which replaces the UB-04 or CMS-1450 billing form. Physicians submit claims via the 837P electronic format, which takes the place of the CMS-1500 billing form. (See figures 1.2 and 1.3.)

Accounts Receivable

The Accounts Receivable department manages the amounts owed to a facility by customers who received services but whose payment will be made at a later date by the patient or his or her third-party payer. Once the claim is submitted to the third-party payer for reimbursement, the accounts receivable clock begins to tick. Typical performance statistics maintained by the Accounts Receivable department include days in accounts receivable and aging of accounts. Days in accounts receivable is calculated by dividing the ending accounts receivable balance for a given period by the average revenue per day. Facilities typically set performance goals for this standard. Aging of accounts is maintained in 30-day increments (0 to 30 days, 31 to 60 days, and so forth). Facilities monitor the number of accounts and the total dollar value in each

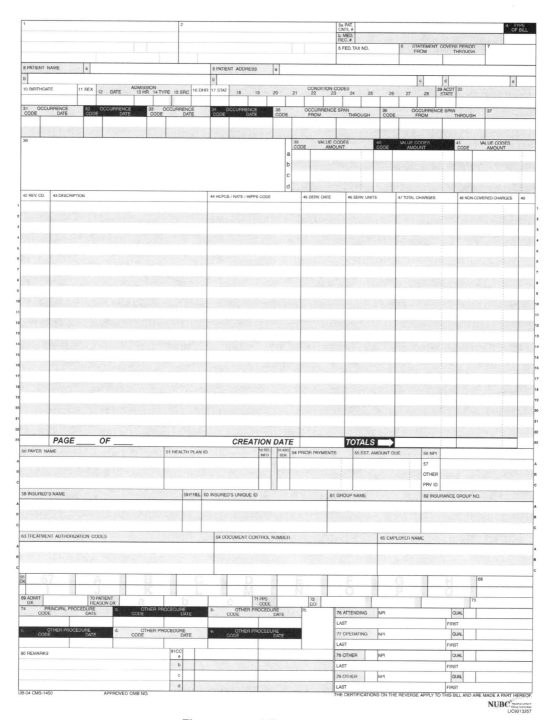

Figure 1.2.   UB-04 claim form

1500

HEALTH INSURANCE CLAIM FORM

APPROVED BY NATIONAL UNIFORM CLAIM COMMITTEE 08/05

CARRIER

□□ PICA   PICA □□

1. MEDICARE	MEDICAID	TRICARE CHAMPUS	CHAMPVA	GROUP HEALTH PLAN	FECA BLK LUNG	OTHER	1a. INSURED'S I.D. NUMBER (For Program in Item 1)
□ (Medicare #)	□ (Medicaid #)	□ (Sponsor's SSN)	□ (Member ID#)	□ (SSN or ID)	□ (SSN)	□ (ID)	

2. PATIENT'S NAME (Last Name, First Name, Middle Initial)

3. PATIENT'S BIRTH DATE MM DD YY   SEX M □ F □

4. INSURED'S NAME (Last Name, First Name, Middle Initial)

5. PATIENT'S ADDRESS (No., Street)

6. PATIENT RELATIONSHIP TO INSURED   Self □ Spouse □ Child □ Other □

7. INSURED'S ADDRESS (No., Street)

CITY   STATE

8. PATIENT STATUS   Single □ Married □ Other □

CITY   STATE

ZIP CODE   TELEPHONE (Include Area Code) ( )

Employed □   Full-Time Student □   Part-Time Student □

ZIP CODE   TELEPHONE (Include Area Code) ( )

9. OTHER INSURED'S NAME (Last Name, First Name, Middle Initial)

10. IS PATIENT'S CONDITION RELATED TO:

11. INSURED'S POLICY GROUP OR FECA NUMBER

a. OTHER INSURED'S POLICY OR GROUP NUMBER

a. EMPLOYMENT? (Current or Previous) YES □ NO □

a. INSURED'S DATE OF BIRTH MM DD YY   SEX M □ F □

b. OTHER INSURED'S DATE OF BIRTH MM DD YY   SEX M □ F □

b. AUTO ACCIDENT?   PLACE (State) YES □ NO □

b. EMPLOYER'S NAME OR SCHOOL NAME

c. EMPLOYER'S NAME OR SCHOOL NAME

c. OTHER ACCIDENT? YES □ NO □

c. INSURANCE PLAN NAME OR PROGRAM NAME

d. INSURANCE PLAN NAME OR PROGRAM NAME

10d. RESERVED FOR LOCAL USE

d. IS THERE ANOTHER HEALTH BENEFIT PLAN? YES □ NO □ If yes, return to and complete item 9 a-d.

READ BACK OF FORM BEFORE COMPLETING & SIGNING THIS FORM.
12. PATIENT'S OR AUTHORIZED PERSON'S SIGNATURE I authorize the release of any medical or other information necessary to process this claim. I also request payment of government benefits either to myself or to the party who accepts assignment below.

SIGNED _____ DATE _____

13. INSURED'S OR AUTHORIZED PERSON'S SIGNATURE I authorize payment of medical benefits to the undersigned physician or supplier for services described below.

SIGNED _____

PATIENT AND INSURED INFORMATION

14. DATE OF CURRENT: MM DD YY ◄ ILLNESS (First symptom) OR INJURY (Accident) OR PREGNANCY(LMP)

15. IF PATIENT HAS HAD SAME OR SIMILAR ILLNESS. GIVE FIRST DATE MM DD YY

16. DATES PATIENT UNABLE TO WORK IN CURRENT OCCUPATION FROM MM DD YY   TO MM DD YY

17. NAME OF REFERRING PROVIDER OR OTHER SOURCE

17a.
17b. NPI

18. HOSPITALIZATION DATES RELATED TO CURRENT SERVICES FROM MM DD YY   TO MM DD YY

19. RESERVED FOR LOCAL USE

20. OUTSIDE LAB? YES □ NO □ $ CHARGES

21. DIAGNOSIS OR NATURE OF ILLNESS OR INJURY (Relate Items 1, 2, 3 or 4 to Item 24E by Line)

1. |___.___| 3. |___.___|

2. |___.___| 4. |___.___|

22. MEDICAID RESUBMISSION CODE   ORIGINAL REF. NO.

23. PRIOR AUTHORIZATION NUMBER

24. A. DATE(S) OF SERVICE From MM DD YY To MM DD YY	B. PLACE OF SERVICE	C. EMG	D. PROCEDURES, SERVICES, OR SUPPLIES (Explain Unusual Circumstances) CPT/HCPCS	MODIFIER	E. DIAGNOSIS POINTER	F. $ CHARGES	G. DAYS OR UNITS	H. EPSDT Family Plan	I. ID. QUAL	J. RENDERING PROVIDER ID. #
1										NPI
2										NPI
3										NPI
4										NPI
5										NPI
6										NPI

25. FEDERAL TAX I.D. NUMBER   SSN □ EIN □

26. PATIENT'S ACCOUNT NO.

27. ACCEPT ASSIGNMENT? (For govt. claims, see back) YES □ NO □

28. TOTAL CHARGE $

29. AMOUNT PAID $

30. BALANCE DUE $

31. SIGNATURE OF PHYSICIAN OR SUPPLIER INCLUDING DEGREES OR CREDENTIALS (I certify that the statements on the reverse apply to this bill and are made a part thereof.)

SIGNED _____ DATE _____

32. SERVICE FACILITY LOCATION INFORMATION

a. NPI   b.

33. BILLING PROVIDER INFO & PH # ( )

a. NPI   b.

PHYSICIAN OR SUPPLIER INFORMATION

NUCC Instruction Manual available at: www.nucc.org

APPROVED OMB-0938-0999 FORM CMS-1500 (08/05)

Figure 1.3   CMS-1500 claim form

increment. The older the account or the longer the account remains unpaid, the less of a chance that the facility will receive reimbursement for the encounter.

Insurance Processing

Once a claim is received by the third-party payer (TPP), the insurance processing of the claim begins. Medicare claims for Part A and Part B services are submitted to a designated Medicare Administrative Contractor (MAC). MACs are replacing the claims payment contractors known as Fiscal Intermediaries (FIs) and Medicare carriers. Prior to MAC implementation, FIs processed Part A claims and some Part B claims, while Medicare carriers processed Part B claims. MACs contract with Medicare to process claims for a specific area or region. MACs serve as the providers' primary point-of-contact for the receipt, processing, and payment of claims. They also perform all core claims processing operations for both Parts A and B (CMS 2006).

Benefits Statements

In addition to processing the claim for payment, TPPs prepare an explanation of benefits (EOB) that is delivered to the patient. The EOB is a statement that describes services rendered, payment covered, and benefit limits and denials. Specifically for Medicare patients, claims payment contractors prepare Medicare Summary Notices (MSNs). The MSN details amounts billed by the provider, amounts approved by Medicare, how much Medicare reimbursed the provider, and what the patient must pay the provider by way of deductible and copayments. EOBs and MSNs are part of the Transactions Rule and are provided to the facility via electronic data interchange (EDI) and are sent to the patient via postal mail.

Remittance Advice

Once the claim is processed by the TPP, a remittance advice (RA) is electronically returned to the provider via the 835A or 835B electronic format. Payments are typically made in batches with the RA sent to the facility and payments electronically transferred to the provider's bank. The RA reports claim rejections, denials, and payments to the facility via EDI.

Claims Reconciliation and Collections

The last component of the revenue cycle is reconciliation and collections. The healthcare facility uses the EOB and RA to reconcile accounts. EOBs identify the amount owed by the patient to the facility. Collections can contact the patient to collect outstanding deductibles and copayments. RAs indicate rejected or denied line items or claims. Facilities can review the RAs and determine whether the claim error can be corrected and resubmitted for additional payment. If a correction is not warranted, reconciliation can be made via a write-off or adjustment to the patient's account. Once the account has been settled, the revenue cycle is completed.

Revenue Cycle Key Performance Indicators

Many facilities have adopted revenue cycle key performance indicators (KPIs) to monitor the performance of their revenue cycle. By using KPIs the facility can pinpoint areas of weakness and work to improve processes and procedures. The Healthcare Financial Management Association (HFMA) KPI Task Force has published a set of KPIs that they recommend for use by facilities across the United States, which is shown in figure 1.4. A complete and accurate CDM directly impacts one KPI: Days in Total Discharged Not Final Billed (DNFB). This trending indicator measures the effectiveness of the claim generation process. If there are issues with data transfer between the CDM and the patient claim, then the days in DNFB can be impacted.

Current CDM Uses

Claim Production

The primary function of the CDM is to produce hospital claims. It is used to translate services rendered to the patient into the data elements required for reporting that service on the hospital claim. The required data elements for claim production will be discussed in detail in chapter 2 of this text. Without the CDM, a clerk would have to manually enter data elements into the claim form for each claim. With the use of the CDM the data elements can be transferred to the claim form electronically and with speed and consistency that manual data entry cannot ensure.

Pricing

The majority of Americans wonders how hospitals set the price or charge for a medical service. Pricing strategies will be discussed in chapter 8 of this text. It is the CDM that houses the charge or price per unit or service. The charge or price is transferred to the hospital claim along with the other required claim data elements. Again, having the charge or price as a component of the CDM allows the charge or price per service to be electronically sent to the claim form in a consistent manner.

Utilization Management

Each time a unit of service is transferred to a patient claim, the CDM tracks the usage of that service. Therefore, at any given time the number of services performed or the number of units of rendered services can be calculated. This is very helpful for utilization management. The Radiology department may want to track how many chest x-rays are performed per month. Further, the department manager wants to confirm that every chest x-ray procedure was billed. The department will most likely have internal records of the number of x-rays performed by month, but comparing that volume with the units of service billed according to the CDM will allow the Radiology department to identify if there is a charge capture issue.

Metric Description		
Measure	**Purpose**	**Value**
Net Days in Accounts Receivable (A/R)	Trending indicator of overall A/R performance	Indicates revenue cycle (RC) efficiency
Aged A/R as a Percentage of Billed A/R	Trending indicator of receivable collectibility	Indicates RC's ability to liquidate A/R
Point-of-Service (POS) Cash Collections	Trending indicator of point-of-service collection efforts	Indicates potential exposure to bad debt, accelerates cash collections, and can reduce collection costs
Cost to Collect	Trending indicator of operational performance	Indicates the efficiency and productivity of RC process
Cash Collection as a Percentage of Adjusted Net Patient Services Revenue	Trending indicator of RC to convert net patient services revenue to cash	Indicates fiscal integrity/financial health of the organization
Bad Debt	Trending indicator of the effectiveness of self-pay collection efforts and financial counseling	Indicates organizations ability to collect self-pay accounts and identifying payer sources for those who can't meet financial obligations
Charity Care	Trending indicator of local ability to pay	Indicates services provided to patients deemed unable to pay
Days in Total Discharged Not Final Billed (DNFB)	Trending indicator of claims generation process	Indicates RC performance and can identify performance issues impacting cash flow

Key:

RC = Revenue Cycle   ATB = Aged Trial Balance Sheet
A/R = Account Receivable   DNFB = Discharged Not Final Bill
BS = Balance sheet   HIM = Health Information Management
IS = Income Statement

Figure 1.4.   HFMA revenue cycle key performance indicator (KPI) definitions

Metric Calculation			
Equation	**Variable Notes**	**Data Source**	**Frequency**
Net A/R	1) Excludes credit balances, non-patient A/R-related third-party settlements and non-patient A/R	BS	Monthly
Net Patient Service Revenue	1) Most recent three-month daily average	IS	
> 30, > 60, > 90, >120 days	1) Aged from discharge date 2) Includes all active billed debit balance accounts (Self-pay commercial, third party) 3) Excludes DNFB and in house accounts	ATB	Monthly
Total A/R	1) No applicable notes	BS	
POS Payments	1) Patient payments collected prior to or up to seven days after discharge 2) Current encounter only 3) Does not include cash collected on prior encounters	A/R	Monthly
Total Patient Cash Collected	1) No applicable notes	A/R	
Total RC Cost	1) Total RC cost includes: software expense, subscription fees, fringe benefits, collection agency fees, outsourced arrangements, patient access expense, patient accounting expense, and HIM expense 2) Patient access includes: eligibility, insurance verification, central scheduling, pre-registration, admissions/registration, and financial counseling	IS	Monthly
Total Cash Collected	1) Cash collected must match the same time frame as cost in the numerator	BS	
Cash Collected	1) Use the current month's cash collected	BS	Monthly
Average Net Revenue	1) Use prior three months, average net revenue 2) Average net revenue is defined as patient service net revenue less bad debt	IS	
Bad Debt Write-Off	1) Expressed as a percentage	IS	Monthly
Gross Patient Service Revenue	1) No applicable notes	IS	
Charity Care Write-Off	1) Expressed as a percentage	IS	Monthly
Gross Patient Service Revenue	1) No applicable notes	IS	
Gross Days in A/R (Not Final Billed)	1) Includes inpatient and outpatient 2) Excludes inhouse claims 3) Only days not final billed 4) Expressed in days	Unbilled A/R	Monthly
Average Daily Gross Revenue	From reporting month	IS	

hfma
healthcare financial management association

Figure 1.4 (continued).

Resource Consumption

Like utilization management, the resource consumption level can be monitored in a consistent and communicable manner with the help of the CDM. The CDM, by using standardized code sets, allows a facility to track the type of services utilized by a specific patient population. For example, the cardiac catheterization unit wants to know what drugs were given to patients who underwent catheterization in May. By using the charge identifier for cardiac catheterization procedures, the department can pull line item level detail from the facility's data warehouse. The department can then analyze the data to determine which types of resources are most often consumed by patients. The department may be particularly interested in recovery room time. Because recovery room time is reported on claims, the service has a unique charge identifier. Therefore, the analysis would be able to determine the average length of time that patients spend in the recovery room post procedure. This is important not only for cost determination but also for staffing and patient scheduling considerations. With the use of CDM data elements, this review can be performed by a data analyst very easily. This is in contrast to requiring a data abstraction professional to review medical records, which can be a very time consuming process.

Oversight

Traditionally, the CDM is housed in the Finance department. However, many clinical and ancillary areas share in the maintenance responsibility. Nonetheless, the CDM Coordinator typically reports to a Finance management team member. Of course there are different models available for use. Some facilities have moved the responsibility to the HIM department because of the strong coding background of many HIM professionals.

CDM Unit

The size of the CDM unit or team will vary from facility to facility. The number of full-time equivalents (FTEs) in the unit depends on the size of the CDM as well as how many facility satellite areas require CDM line item management. Typically, there is a CDM Coordinator position that manages the CDM unit. CDM Coordinator position requirements vary from facility to facility based on the philosophy and complexity of CDM management of the facility. In general, the following are qualifications that CDM Coordinators should possess:

Considerable knowledge of the revenue cycle

Good communication skills, both verbal and written

Basic understanding, if not advanced understanding, of coding and reimbursement systems

Management experience

The CDM Coordinator position is one of great importance. Even though this is a very detail-oriented position, the coordinator must also be able to engage others in the maintenance process. Individuals interested in this position must be able to strike a balance between control and delegation—not always an easy task.

HIM–CDM Connection

Though the CDM function has been, and continues to be, housed primarily in the Finance department at many facilities, HIM professionals have an important role in the maintenance of the CDM. The coding and reimbursement experience of CDM coordinators varies from hospital to hospital. Therefore, the coding and reimbursement expertise of HIM professionals is often sought after by the CDM team. The HIM professional may assist the CDM team with understanding the intent of a CPT/HCPCS code, may help the CDM team understand new coding guidelines released for a CPT code, may assist the CDM team with understanding how new CMS regulations impact the CDM, and may assist the CDM team with communicating coding rules and regulations to various clinical or ancillary department managers.

Additionally, it is valuable for the HIM department and CDM team to have a good working relationship. By exploring each professional's roles and responsibilities they will see that they may have more in common than they thought. By working together and understanding each other's roles, the two units have a major impact on key performance indicators established for the revenue cycle, thus improving the efficiency of providing quality service for all patients.

Summary

From a paper list to a large database, the CDM has significantly evolved over the past several years. The care and maintenance of the CDM is a very important task, not to be taken lightly. Being a member of a CDM team is very challenging but extremely rewarding. As a crucial member of the revenue cycle, the CDM team execution of their roles and responsibilities will help their facility to achieve financial success. Appendix A contains a sample job description for a Chargemaster coordinator.

References

Casto, A. and E. Layman. 2010. *Principles of Healthcare Reimbursement*, 3rd ed. Chicago: AHIMA.

Centers for Medicare and Medicaid Services. 2003. HIPAA Information Series: HIPAA 101 for Health Providers' Offices. http://www.cms.gov/EducationMaterials/Downloads/HIPAA101-1.pdf.

Centers for Medicare and Medicaid Services. 2006. CMS Introduction to Medicare Contracting Reform. http://www.humtech.com/cms/mcrpublic/.

Centers for Medicare and Medicaid Services. 2008. Admission and Registration Requirements. Chapter 2 in Medicare Claims Processing Manual. http://www.cms.gov/manuals/downloads/clm104c02.pdf.

Department of Health and Human Services. 2003 (February 20). Health Insurance Reform: Modifications to Electronic Data Transaction Standards and Code Sets. *Federal Register* 68(34):8381–8399.

HFMA KPI Task Force. 2010. Leveraging KPI Use for Revenue Cycle Success. *hfm (Healthcare Financial Management)*, 64(1):31–34.

Resources

Bohley, M. and B. Kost. 2005. Beyond APCs: New challenges with outpatient coding, compliance, and reimbursement. Do you know where you stand? *Proceedings of AHIMA's 77th National Convention and Exhibit.* Chicago: AHIMA.

Grzybowski, D. and L. Schraffenberger. 2006. Double duty: Where HIM and chargemaster coding intersect. *Proceedings of AHIMA's 78th National Convention and Exhibit Proceedings.* Chicago: AHIMA.

Kuehn, L and L. Schraffenberger. 2009. *Effective Management of Coding Services*, 4th ed. Chicago: AHIMA.

Chapter 2

Charge Description Master Structure

Anne B. Casto, RHIA, CCS

Although each CDM is unique to a hospital or hospital system, there are standard data elements that are included in each CDM. Each of these elements is defined in this chapter, and their use and importance to the claim production process are also discussed.

Charge Code

The charge code, also known as service code, charge description number, or charge identifier, is a hospital-specific, internally assigned code used to identify an item or service. The code is typically numeric; however, that is dependent upon the hospital's own CDM strategy or structure.

Charge code numbers are assigned or distributed by a designated person, IT department, or the CDM coordinator. The methodology for distribution depends on the facility. Similar to typical medical record number schemes, the charge code number may be distributed in straight numerical order, or a facility may reserve numerical sections by ancillary service. For example, charge code number set 100000–199999 is reserved for radiology.

Regardless of the distribution methodology, each charge code number must be unique. Therefore, the CDM unit must ensure that there are not duplicate charge codes in the CDM. The CDM Coordinator should schedule and complete duplicate charge code audits throughout the year.

Department Code

Department code is a hospital-specific number that is assigned to each clinical or ancillary department that provides services to patients and has at least one charge item in the CDM. Alternative terminology for this data element may be general ledger number. This code is used to identify the area within the healthcare facility that is providing

Table 2.1. Combination of department code and service code to create unique charge code

Department Code	Venipuncture Service Code	Unique Charge Code
123 – Emergency department	12345	12312345
124 - Clinic	12345	12412345
125 – Pre-operative holding	12345	12512345

the service. The codes usually correspond with an ancillary or clinical service such as speech therapy or by physical area such as Emergency department.

Some facilities accomplish having multiple charge items for the same service that are performed in different areas by combining the department number and a service code to create the unique charge code. For example, venipunctures are often performed in various areas for the healthcare facility and are a prime candidate for this type of structure. Table 2.1 provides an illustration of this methodology. By using this methodology, charge entry users within the healthcare facility can look at the unique charge code and know that the venipuncture (12345) was performed in the Emergency department (123) when the charge code 12312345 appears on the claim.

Revenue Code

A revenue code is a four-digit numeric code that is required for billing on the UB-04 claim form or the 8371 ETS. Revenue codes are maintained by the National Uniform Billing Committee. Therefore, revenue codes are standard, and the same code set is utilized by all facilities. What vary from facility to facility are the services or CPT/HCPCS codes that are assigned to a revenue code or code group. However, revenue code assignment is usually driven by the ancillary department or location where the service was rendered. Revenue code reporting requirements for Medicare are detailed in the Medicare Claims Processing Manual, Chapter 25, Section 75.4 (CMS 2005). At each facility the revenue code reported on individual claims is utilized at the end-of-year cost reporting process.

Although the revenue code list is standardized, the combination of CPT/HCPCS code and revenue code can be somewhat facility specific. However, Medicare and other third-party payers issue transmittals and bulletins that provide revenue code instruction for use with specific CPT/HCPCS codes. Additionally, the Medicare Code Editor (MCE) and the Integrated Outpatient Code Editor (IOCE) used by the Medicare Administrative Contractors (MACs) contain revenue code and CPT/HCPCS code edits to ensure that appropriate combinations are reported on the claim when required. Appendix B contains a list of Medicare revenue codes.

In addition to identifying the service area or type of service performed, revenue codes are used by third-party payers to identify payment methodologies for specific services in their contracts. Therefore, the use of revenue codes for services must be reviewed very closely by the hospital contract management team. For example, consider the following contract language for three payers at a facility. Payer one indicates in the contract that he or she will pay 60 percent of billed charges for MRI services identified by revenue code 0610. The second payer, Medicare, specifies that the most specific revenue code be used for MRI services and facilities should report the applicable code in range 0610–0614. The third payer specifies that he or she will reimburse MRI services based on the CPT code regardless of the revenue code used. The CDM unit must work closely with hospital contract managers to ensure that the CDM is meeting the reporting needs for all three of these payers, not just major payers like Medicare.

CPT/HCPCS Code

CPT/HCPCS code is the current code assigned by the American Medical Association (AMA) and CMS to be reported for individual services, procedures, and supplies rendered to the patient. Code use requirements may be payer-specific, namely Medicare, Medicaid, Blue Cross, and the like. It is important to remember that CPT/HCPCS codes are not provided for all line items. Several services or supplies billed to the patient do not have associated CPT/HCPCS codes (room rates, general supplies) and, therefore, this data element will be blank for these line items.

The CPT/HCPCS code delineates several data pieces within the charge item. The CPT/HCPCS code sets were established by the Health Insurance Portability and Accountability Act of 1996 (HIPAA) as the designated code set to be used on certain electronic transactions by all healthcare facilities and insurers for the services, procedures, and supplies rendered in the outpatient settings. Therefore, the use of CPT/HCPCS codes is mandatory when codes are available for reporting.

There are instances where Medicare and other third-party payers may require different codes to report a service. Medicare maintains the HCPCS Level II system that in part contains temporary codes they have developed for use in various Medicare Prospective Payment Systems (PPS). In these instances, the facility must make accommodations in the CDM for both codes for that specific service. Currently, CMS requires different codes for some (but not all) coronary artery stent placement services. CMS has created "G-codes" for hospital outpatient departments to use for Medicare patients as outlined in table 2.2. Other third-party payers may not follow Medicare reporting guidance and require the CPT codes rather than the HCPCS G-codes. Therefore, facilities serving both a Medicare and a commercial patient population must be able to report the correct code for services based on the patient's financial class. Some facilities accomplish this by creating different charge items based on financial class. (See table 2.3.) Other

Table 2.2.   Coronary artery stent placement services CPT/HCPCS codes

Code	Description
92980	Transcatheter placement of an intracoronary stent(s), percutaneous, with or without other therapeutic intervention, any method; single vessel
92981	Transcatheter placement of an intracoronary stent(s), percutaneous, with or without other therapeutic intervention, any method; each additional vessel
G0290	Transcatheter placement of a drug eluting intracoronary stent(s), percutaneous, with or without other therapeutic intervention, any method; single vessel
G0291	Transcatheter placement of a drug eluting intracoronary stent(s), percutaneous, with or without other therapeutic intervention, any method; each additional vessel

Source: AMA 2009; CMS 2010a.

Table 2.3.   Coronary stent placement, drug eluting stent, by payer example 1

Charge Code	Dept. #	Description	HCPCS Code	Rev Code	Charge
12345	301	Coronary stent placement, drug eluting stent—Medicare	G0290	0481	$9,375.00
12346	301	Coronary stent placement, drug eluting stent—non-Medicare	92980	0481	$9,375.00

Table 2.4.   Coronary stent placement, drug eluting stent, by payer example 2

Charge Code	Dept. #	Description	HCPCS Code	HCPCS Code - CMS	Rev Code	Charge
12345	301	Coronary stent placement, drug eluting stent	92980	G0290	0418	$9,375.00

facilities may add a column in the CDM for "Medicare CPT/HCPCS code" as shown in table 2.4. Either way, the facility must have a procedure in place to ensure that the required code is placed on the claim in order to prevent rejections and denials issued by the payer as well as to receive proper reimbursement.

What would happen if a facility reported a coronary drug eluting stent placement with CPT code 92980 rather than G0290 for a Medicare patient? Table 2.5 compares the ambulatory payment classification (APC) assignment as well as APC reimbursement rates for these two codes. If a facility fails to use HCPCS Level II codes as designated by Medicare for drug eluting stent placement, the facility would not receive the correct reimbursement amount; in essence, they would have given up $1,753.21 in reimbursement for the service.

Table 2.5. **APC assignment and reimbursement rates for drug eluting stent placement.**

Code	APC	APC Description	Relative Weight (2010)	Reimbursement Rate (2010)
92980	0104	Transcatheter placement of intracoronary stents	84.7773	$5,714.50
G0290	0656	Transcatheter placement of intracoronary drug eluting stents	110.7870	$7,467.71

Source: AMA 2009; CMS 2010b.

Modifier

Modifiers are codes used by providers and facilities to identify or flag a service that has been modified in some way or to provide more specific information about the procedure or service. There are two sources of modifiers. The first source of modifiers includes those that are part of the CPT code set. The second source of modifiers includes those that are part of the HCPCS Level II code set.

Because the use of a modifier can alter the meaning of the code in some way, it is important that modifiers are only applied to CPT and HCPCS codes when documentation in the medical record supports the application of the modifier. Therefore, hard-coding of modifiers in the CDM is rare, but some facilities do utilize this practice. CDM units should pay close attention to modifier reporting guidelines if they choose to hard-code a modifier into the CDM. CDM units should consider all compliance implications that could arise due to the hard-coded modifier appearing with the associated CPT/HCPCS code every time the charge code is activated by the order entry process.

Charge Description

Charge description is an explanatory phrase that has been assigned to describe the procedure, service, or supply. The charge description is usually based on the official CPT/HCPCS description when applicable, but the field is often limited by the character length allowed by the financial system, so shorter descriptions are utilized.

The AMA and CMS provide an official long description for each code. Additionally, a short description is provided for use in space-limited fields within hospital systems. The CDM team must decide if the short description of the code should be used as the hospital description or if a modified description would better suit their facility. Likewise, a list of commonly used abbreviations should be maintained in order to provide consistency through the CDM. The dilemma lies in the fact that most practitioners are not familiar with the official CPT/HCPCS code description; rather, they use working lay titles for the procedures and services they perform or provide. Therefore, using the official short descriptions in the computerized or manual order entry system or CDM may be confusing for the service providers. On the flip side, consumers of healthcare may better understand the official short or long description than the lay term used by practitioners. As hospitals work to improve customer service with their patients, they are striving to produce a patient bill that the patient can easily comprehend.

To illustrate this point, compare a few lay descriptions to some official short descriptions that are located in table 2.6. In examples A and B, do you think the average patient would be able identify the service they received from the charge description? If you did not know coding, would you know what "SLP treatment" represents? It is likely that only ancillary therapists may understand the hospital lay description for these therapy services. Likewise, in examples C and D perhaps only radiology technicians, radiologists, physicians, and coders may understand the hospital lay descriptions for these services. Do you think that the average patient would be able to connect "SP Arterio Renal Bilateral" to the catheterization that they received? What description would be even more patient friendly for examples B and D?

There are no hard and fast rules regarding the description that must be used in the CDM charge description field. Each facility must determine which methodology works best for their facility. The Healthcare Financial Management Association (HFMA) published significant work in the area of patient-friendly billing. HFMA has launched the Patient Friendly Billing project (HFMA 2010a) to encourage facilities to improve billing for patients. The philosophy of the project is based on the following ideals:

- The needs of patients and family members should be paramount when designing administrative processes and communications.

Table 2.6.   Sample charge descriptions (lay descriptions) versus official short descriptions

Example	Charge Description	Code	Official Short Description
A	SLP treatment	92507	Speech/hearing therapy
B	CPM set-up	97001	PT evaluation
C	Treatment aids-interm	77333	Radiation treatment aid(s); intermediate
D	SP arterio renal bilateral	36246	Place catheter in artery; initial second order

Source: AMA 2009; CMS 2010b.

- Information gathering should be coordinated with other providers and insurers, and this collection process should be done efficiently, privately, and with as little duplication as possible.

- When possible, communication of financial information should not occur during the medical encounter.

- *The average reader should easily understand the language and format of financial communications.*

- Continuous improvement of the billing process should be made by implementing better practices and incorporating feedback from patients and consumers (HFMA 2010b).

Though many revenue cycle areas are impacted by this project, it is clear that there is emphasis on the charge descriptions used by facilities on the patient bill. Visit the HFMA Web site to find out more about the Patient Friendly Billing Project and to locate guidance and advice on this topic.

Charge (Price)

The charge or price is the dollar amount the hospital is charging for the item or service rendered to the patient. Hospital charging methodologies have recently come under close scrutiny by the American public; specifically, how facilities charge self-insured and uninsured patients. Additionally, in the Final Rule for Inpatient Prospective Payment System FY 2007 Update (HHS 2006), Medicare discusses its plan for Healthcare Transparency, or how it plans to provide the American public with healthcare cost and quality data to initiate interest in choosing the best provider at the best price. Healthcare transparency and charging methodologies will be discussed in detail in chapter 8 of this text.

Though the charge itself is a data element within the CDM, the Finance department within the healthcare facility typically manages this data element. Statistics gathered from the CDM may be useful in analyzing charge structure. Likewise, oddities that are identified should be investigated by the revenue cycle team, but the actual setting of rates is typically not performed by the CDM team.

Charge Status (Active or Inactive)

Charge status is an identifier used to indicate if a line item charge is currently being used by the facility to report a service or supply. Hospitals may or may not maintain an active indicator status in the CDM. Most facilities will not delete charge items from their CDM in order to preserve historic practices, and therefore, use a charge status indicator instead. This allows the facility to maintain the integrity of charge items that have been used in the past and may be reviewed at later dates by Medicare and other third-party payers. It is also a way to identify whether new charge items are needed. In the charge item addition process, the requested charge item can be compared to inactive charge items. If there is a match, the appropriate discussions can then take place about why the charge item was moved to inactive status and to determine whether the new charge is necessary.

Payer Identifier

Payer identifier codes are used to differentiate among payers that may have specific or special billing protocol in place. Illustration of this practice was described in the CPT/ HCPCS code section. It is important for the CDM team to review the payer identifier assignment on a regular basis. Each time a payer contract is revised, the CDM team must work with the contract management unit to determine if changes in payer identifier assignment are warranted.

For example, a facility's largest payer (Super Payer) is adopting the CMS Outpatient Prospective Payment System (OPPS) methodology. Previously, Super Payer paid a percent of charge and did not require facilities to use HCPCS Level II codes. However, with the movement to OPPS, now they will require HCPCS Level II codes and the Super Payer is adopting the same reporting requirements as Medicare. The payer identifier assignment for Super Payer may need to be revisited prior to the switch in their methodology as displayed in table 2.7.

Table 2.7.   Example of impact on payer identifier by payer reimbursement methodology change

Super Payer – Reimbursement Methodology is Percent of Billed Charges						
Charge Code	Dept. #	Description	HCPCS Code	HCPCS Code – CMS	Rev Code	Charge
12345	301	Coronary stent placement, drug eluting stent	92980	G0290	0418	$9,375.00
Super Payer – Reimbursement Methodology is OPPS						
Charge Code	Dept. #	Description	HCPCS Code	HCPCS Code – CMS and Super Payer	Rev Code	Charge
12345	301	Coronary stent placement, drug eluting stent	92980	G0290	0418	$9,375.00

Table 2.8.   Sample CDM

Charge Code	Dept Code	Rev-enue Code	CPT/ HCPCS Code	Modi-fier**	Charge Descrip-tion	Charge*	Charge Status (A/I)	Payer ID**
1238571	123	450	99281		Level 1 ED	$100.00	A	
1238572	123	450	99282		Level 2 ED	$200.00	A	
1238573	123	450	99283		Level 3 ED	$300.00	A	
1238574	123	450	99284		Level 4 ED	$400.00	A	
1238575	123	450	99285		Level 5 ED	$500.00	A	

* Charge is fictitious and should not be used for benchmarking or rate setting
** Intentionally blank, modifier and special payer designation not applicable

Summary

Each facility will have a unique design and philosophy for their CDM. However, each design must incorporate the required billing data elements. Table 2.8 provides an excerpt from a sample CDM. Regardless of the structure adopted by the facility, the CDM unit will need to design maintenance processes to keep the CDM complete and accurate. CDM maintenance and CDM workflows are discussed in chapters 3 and 4 of this text.

References

American Medical Association. 2009. *Current Procedural Terminology,* 4th ed. Chicago: American Medical Association.

Centers for Medicare and Medicaid Services. 2005. Overview. http://www.cms.gov/Manuals/01_Overview.asp.

Centers for Medicare and Medicaid Services. 2010a. Healthcare Procedure Coding System (HCPCS) Level II.

Centers for Medicare and Medicaid Services. 2010b. Addendum B.-OPPS Payment by HCPCS Code for CY 2010. http://www.cms.gov/HospitalOutpatientPPS/AU/list.asp#TopOfPage.

Centers for Medicare and Medicaid Services. 2010c. Medicare Claims Processing Manual. http://www.cms.hhs.gov/Manuals/IOM/list.asp.

Dietz, M. S. 2005 (October). Ensure equitable reimbursement through an accurate charge description master. *Proceedings from AHIMA's 77th National Convention and Exhibit.* Chicago: AHIMA.

Department of Health and Human Services. 2006 (August 18). Revision to hospital inpatient prospective payment systems – 2007 FY occupational mix adjustment to wage index; Implementation; Final Rule. *Federal Register* 71(160):47870–48351.

Healthcare Financial Management Association. 2010a. Patient Friendly Billing. http://www.hfma.org/ HFMA-Initiatives/Patient-Friendly-Billing/Patient-Friendly-Billing/.

Healthcare Financial Management Association. 2010b. Patient Friendly Billing: Purpose and Philosophy. www.hfma.org/library/revenue/PatientFriendlyBilling/purpose.htm.

Leeds, E. 2001 (October). When good chargemasters go bad. *Proceedings from AHIMA's 73rd National Convention and Exhibit.* Chicago: AHIMA.

National Uniform Billing Committee. 2010. http://www.nubc.org.

Chapter 3

Charge Description Master Maintenance

Anne B. Casto, RHIA, CCS

CDM maintenance is an ongoing process at any healthcare facility, physician office, hospital, imaging center, or freestanding laboratory facility. There are numerous events throughout the year that provide cause for CDM maintenance. CPT/HCPCS codes are updated regularly throughout the year, as is billing and coding guidance. Likewise, payer contracts are usually negotiated based on the facility's fiscal year, which may or may not correspond with Medicare's various payment system updates. Understanding the hospital's financial calendar is an important part of planning for ongoing maintenance to the CDM.

Each year the CDM coordinator should ensure that the proper resources are acquired for CDM maintenance. Updated codebooks as well as national, uniform billing data set information are required. Additionally, payer instructions such as the Medicare Claims Processing Manual should be available so that crucial instructions can be easily located and reviewed. Any publications specific to the state in which your facility operates should be present as well (Dietz 2005, 3). Many of these resources are available online. However, your CDM team may consider having a shared location to house the links to these documents to ensure that all team members are able to access the necessary documents without having to spend time searching on the Internet.

Although facilities may utilize different management structures, the CDM unit or team, CDM Committee, or Revenue Cycle Team will need to oversee the CDM maintenance process. The oversight should not be one individual's responsibility as varying perspectives and expertise are required to create a comprehensive plan. One of the major responsibilities of the team is to develop policies and procedures for the CDM review plan (Bielby, et al. 2010). (See Appendix C.) As the CDM team is developing policies and procedures for the CDM maintenance process, they should consider the following questions:

- Do our policies cover how coding and billing regulations are communicated within the organization? Do we expect a response?
- Do our policies address resources and instructions for code updates?
- Do our policies require coders and billers to document any advice received from the Medicare Administrative Contractor?
- Are we addressing CDM risk areas in our policies and procedures?
- Do our policies define how consultants may be used in CDM maintenance? Should they? (Acumentra Health 2005, 11-12).

Once the policies and procedures are in place, the team can start to build their maintenance plan.

Maintenance Plan

CDM maintenance is a very detailed process and must be approached very methodically. Therefore, the maintenance plan should consist of several organized and structured processes, and CDM coordinators may want to consider a project plan approach to CDM maintenance. A CDM maintenance plan will allow all individuals and departments that are included in the maintenance process to understand how their components fit into the larger maintenance plan. Likewise, each participant will understand his or her duties and be fully aware of the expected timeline for completion. Not only does this help individuals stay on task, but it can be very beneficial to new employees who may not be familiar with the facility's internal process.

Working with Hospital Departments

Ancillary and other clinical areas play a large role in CDM maintenance. Their clinical expertise combined with the coding knowledge of the CDM coordinator or HIM representative will allow a facility to have a current, accurate, and complete CDM. It is important to remember that the primary focus of clinical and ancillary areas is patient care. Therefore, the CDM coordinator must engage the departments in the CDM maintenance process.

Understanding Services

Having a good working relationship with clinical and ancillary areas is important for the maintenance process. Who better to explain services, service components, and service delivery techniques than health professionals themselves? Understanding the service is the key to assigning the appropriate CPT or HCPCS code for the charge item. For example, interventional radiology is a very challenging service area for many coders and CDM professionals. This service area requires code selection from both the surgical and radiology sections. Understanding which codes are used together for which procedures is critical. Therefore, having a clinician from the interventional radiology department explain which procedures are performed by the facility and how the components work together is paramount. This type of valuable interaction will provide clinical insight to help ensure that these complex cases are accurately and completely reported by the facility.

Understanding the CDM

As important as it is for clinical and ancillary areas to share their expertise with the CDM coordinator, it is equally as important for the CDM coordinator to explain the compliance or billing implications with the clinical areas. It is much easier to get buy-in from healthcare professionals when they understand the reasoning behind a set process or protocol. Providing an example with significant financial implications is an effective way to help ancillary and clinical professionals understand why proper code selection is vital in the CDM maintenance process. For example, a CDM team member is updating the charge ticket for the neurology clinic. The team member identifies three charge codes with the same description: autonomic nerve function test. The neurology manager may not understand the issue, as the clinical professionals in the clinic understand the difference between tests one, two, and three. However, what if the charge entry clerks do not? Further review of the utilization report for this clinic reveals that the first listed charge code is reported 98 percent of the time. Is that the actual utilization? A sample of medical records are reviewed, and it is determined that the wrong charge code was activated 65 percent of the time. To make matters worse, because the wrong charge code was activated, the wrong CPT code (95921 rather than 95922 or 95923) was reported on the claim for several encounters. Because of the charging error, the facility was overpaid by Medicare for several claims and they must now re-submit the claims with the corrected CPT code and pay back the overpayment amount. How can this be prevented in the future? The CDM team must take the time to work with the neurology clinic manager and revise the charge descriptions so they better differentiate among the three tests. Although similar descriptions may not be an issue for the clinicians, clearly they can be for other hospital staff members. Appreciating the complexities of each other's roles and responsibilities will strengthen the relationship between the CDM team and the clinical and ancillary areas.

Components of a CDM Maintenance Plan

There are numerous maintenance activities in which the CDM team will engage throughout the year. To be able to understand and effectively communicate the intent of the maintenance activities, the CDM team should establish a scope of review for each review. By defining the scope, each participant will understand the intent and extent of the review. The CDM coordinator will be able to communicate what is included and what is not included in each review activity to the Finance team and the revenue cycle team.

Although each facility is different, the following technical activities should be included in the CDM maintenance plan for each review:

- Review of current statistics
- CPT/HCPCS code review
- Revenue code review
- Modifier review (Dietz 2005, 3)

Each of these line item components should be addressed in the review. However, it is not enough to just review each component individually to ensure that it is a valid code. Rather, the whole line item should be reviewed to ensure that the components fit together properly. This is where CDM maintenance can become very complex. The reviewer must ensure that the line item components meet the requirements for each payer as well as meet the requirements established under compliance guidance.

There is so much to remember to research and verify during the CDM maintenance process. Having a thorough review plan is critical. Mapping out each task in the plan will force the reviewer to complete all planned activities. Likewise, it is during this process that the CDM review policies and procedures must be adhered to. The following ethics vignette illustrates the importance of adhering to CDM policies and procedures during the CDM maintenance process.

Miscoding to Avoid Conflicts

Gretchen, a registered health information technician (RHIT) and a clinical coding specialist (CCS), has worked for the Headache and Pain Center for over 10 years. Her job responsibilities include diagnosis and procedure coding for the services provided by the Ambulatory Surgical Center (ASC) owned by a group of anesthesiologists. The physicians routinely provide pain management services to Medicare patients, including epidural injections involving cervical, thoracic, and lumbar vertebrae. Claims forms are submitted to Medicare with CPT4 codes.

Several years ago, Gretchen read in a credible professional coding resource that the CPT book's description had changed recently to reflect only procedures performed on the lumbar region and that there was no longer any valid CPT code for an epidural injection of a steroid into the cervical and thoracic vertebra. Knowing that the physicians sought reimbursement by Medicare for a facility fee when this procedure was performed, she contacted the Medicare provider representative. The representative suggested that she continue to use the CPT for the epidural. She trusted this advice and did not speak to the physicians about her concerns.

Gretchen was somewhat uncomfortable with using a CPT code that did not exactly describe what had been done, but not using the code would make the physicians very angry because no facility payment would be made. To avoid any misunderstanding, she changed the description in the billing system with the codes to reflect cervical epidural injection.

Because the Medicare representative said the coding would be appropriate, she went ahead and billed this way for three years until CPT corrected the problem in 2000. Now, a postpayment review by Medicare has discovered the coding variance and has made the physician return the substantial overpayment for noncovered ASC facility services. The physicians blame Gretchen for miscoding the services and are taking the issue to court.

Source: Harman, L. 2006. *Ethical Challenges in the Management of Health Information.* Sudbury, MA: Jones & Bartlett Learning. 110–113. http://www.jblearning.com. Reprinted with permission.

The responsibility of charge or price setting varies from hospital to hospital. Most often this activity is the responsibility of the Finance department. Therefore, charge or price review may or may not be performed by the CDM team. However, the CDM team can assist the Finance department by identifying charges that appear to be outside of the normal limits. For example, the CDM team could identify all line items that are missing charge or price. Likewise, they could identify line items that have a charge or price lower than the Medicare reimbursement rate under the current OPPS.

Ongoing Maintenance

There are ongoing maintenance activities that the CDM team must complete on a regular basis. There will always be issues that arise and need to be addressed immediately. However, the majority of maintenance can be scheduled and, therefore, staffing of the CDM team for these activities can be projected.

CPT Updates

The CPT Editorial Research and Development department supports the modification process for the CPT code set. The CPT Editorial Panel meets three times per year to consider proposals for changes to CPT (AMA 2010). The Editorial Panel is supported by the CPT Advisory Committee, which is composed of representatives of more than 90 medical specialty societies and other healthcare professional organizations. To stay current with new technologies and pioneering procedures, CPT is revised each year with changes effective the following January 1.

The updated code set is released prior to January 1. Therefore, the CDM maintenance plan should include steps for the acquisition of the new code set as well as adequate time for the additions, deletions, and modifications to be reviewed and incorporated into the CDM as warranted. Certainly this makes December a very busy time of year for the CDM team. The CDM coordinator should give special attention to time-off requests for the CDM team members to ensure that line items will be ready for use by January 1. Additionally, the CDM Coordinator needs to schedule the annual maintenance with IT and other revenue cycle team representatives. Not only do the CDM line items need to be up to date, but the team must ensure that adequate time is provided for IT to update computerized order entry and ensure that CDM to finance system interfaces remain intact. If charge tickets are utilized, the ancillary or clinical units must have adequate time to ensure that the tickets are up to date and staff is properly educated on charge entry changes.

CPT Update

When codes are deleted and new replacement codes are provided during the annual CPT code update, close attention should be paid to the reporting details. For calendar year (CY) 2010, AMA modified a portion of the pain management procedure codes as displayed in the table below.

AMA is moving from using four codes to using six codes to report this injection procedure. Your facility currently provides this service and the CDM contains four line items for reporting purposes. What is your facility's policy and procedure for updating a line item where a code is replaced by two or more code choices? Does your policy allow for the deactivation of all four line items with the creation of six new line items? Does your policy require that the four current line items be updated with the new CPT codes and then two additional line items be created for the remaining two CPT codes?

What about pricing? Does the Finance department simply adopt the current pricing scheme and apply it to the new line items? Close attention to the code instruction for the new codes provides valuable information for the charge or price setting for the new codes. There is a INCLUDES code for codes 64490–64495, which indicates that image guidance (CT or fluoroscopy) and any contrast injection is included in the code. Previously, under the 2009 code set (64470–64476) imaging was separately reported with radiology code 77003. The Finance department must now determine how to incorporate the charge for the imaging component into the charge for the injection procedure.

Once the technical update to the line items is completed, a review of how the codes should be reported must be addressed with the clinical area. Again, the education must go beyond the fact that there are new codes for this portion of the pain management procedures. Close attention must be paid to the instructional guidance provided for the code sets. There is an instruction note provided under codes 64492 and 64495 indicating that the facility should not report these codes more than one time per day. That is these codes have a maximum unit of one. This is new guidance as codes 64472 and 64476 did not have unit guidance in 2009. Education should be provided to charge entry staff to ensure that they understand that each of the codes in this code set (64490–64495) has a unit maximum of one. This holds true even if four spinal levels are treated. (see table).

2009 – Injection Procedure Reporting for Four Cervical Levels

Charge Identifier	Revenue Code	CPT Code	Description	Unit
361234	0360	64470	Inj, paravertebral jt, cervical single level	1
361235	0360	64472	Inj, paravertebral jt, cervical second and add level	3
321257	0320	77003	Fluoroscopic guidance	1

2010 – Injection Procedure Reporting for Four Cervical Levels

Charge Identifier	Revenue Code	CPT Code	Description	Unit
362345	0360	64490	Inj, paravertebral jt, cervical single level	1
362346	0360	64491	Inj, paravertebral jt, cervical second level	1
362347	0360	64492	Inj, paravertebral jt, cervical third and add level	1

Additionally, as mentioned above, the new code set 64490–64495 includes the imaging guidance and the contrast injection. These services should no longer be separately reported. The order entry staff must be educated on this charge entry change. Further, the staff needs to understand that not all pain management codes have changed. The code set of 64479–64484 has not been modified in the same way as 64470–64476 and continues to require the imaging guidance (77003) to be separately reported.

HCPCS Level II Updates

Permanent HCPCS Level II codes are maintained by the CMS HCPCS workgroup. Permanent national codes are updated annually every January 1. Temporary codes can be added, changed, or deleted on a quarterly basis (Casto and Layman 2010).

Like the CPT code updates, the HCPCS Level II code updates must be planned for as well. But in addition to the yearly updates, CDM coordinators must plan for quarterly updates to the temporary HCPCS Level II codes as well. See tables 3.1 and 3.2 for listings of permanent and temporary HCPCS Level II codes.

Table 3.1.   Permanent HCPCS codes

Permanent Code Categories	Covers	Insurers
A codes	Ambulance and transportation services, medical and surgical supplies, administrative, and miscellaneous and investigational services and supplies	All payers
B codes	Enteral and parenteral therapy	All payers
D codes	Dental	All payers
E codes	Durable medical equipment	All payers
J codes	Drugs that cannot ordinarily be self-administered, chemotherapy, immunosuppressive drugs, inhalation solutions	All payers
L codes	Orthotic and prosthetic procedures and devices	All payers
M codes	Office services and cardiovascular and other medical services	All payers
P codes	Pathology and laboratory services	All payers
R codes	Diagnostic radiology	All payers
V codes	Vision, hearing, and speech-language pathology services	All payers

Source: CMS 2010.

Table 3.2.   Temporary HCPCS codes

Temporary Code Categories	Covers	Insurers
C codes	Items that may qualify for pass-through payment under HOPPS	Medicare hospital outpatient claims
G codes	Professional health care procedures and services	Medicare hospital outpatient claims
Q codes	Drugs, biologicals, medical equipment	Medicare hospital outpatient claims
K codes	Durable medical equipment	DME MACs—Durable Medical Equipment Medicare Administrative Contractors
S codes	Drugs, services, and supplies	Medicaid and private insurers
H codes	Mental health services	State Medicaid agencies
T codes	Items for which there are no permanent national codes	State Medicaid agencies and private insurers

Source: CMS 2010.

HCPCS Level II code updates require coordination with a variety of areas in the healthcare facility. Not only does the code set contain procedure or service codes, but also included are drug codes, supply codes, durable medical equipment (DME) codes, and implantable device codes. The CDM team must work closely with materials management and the Pharmacy department to ensure that the CDM line items properly represent the drugs, biologicals, and devices utilized by the facility.

HCPCS Level II Update, part 1

During the HCPCS Level II update it is important to review codes that are recycled or reinstated in HCPCS Level II. For CY 2009, CMS reinstated code J1750, injection, iron dextran, 50 mg. This code was previously used through December 31, 2005. In 2006, two new codes were activated for iron dextran: J1751, iron dextran 165 and J1752, iron dextran 267 for use through December 31, 2008.

In order to determine if the charge item data elements previously active in the CDM are still applicable today it is important to review processes from 2006. For example, what CDM maintenance approach did your CDM team use during the 2006 HCPCS Level II update? There may or may not be documentation. So now your investigative work begins. Was the charge item with code J1750 deactivated or deleted and two new charge items with codes J1751 and J1752 added? Was the charge item with code J1750 modified so that it now included code J1751 and then a new charge item was added for J1752? Once you have determined what happened in the past, how will your facility handle the reinstatement? Do you have a policy or procedure in place?

What about the charge or price? Does your facility charge different amounts for J1751 and J1752? Now that your facility must go back to one HCPCS Level II code for both types of iron dextran, J1750, what will the charge or price be?

The CDM team must work closely with the Pharmacy department to ensure that the active code is included in both the pharmacy order entry system and the CDM with the appropriate data elements and dosage information. The pharmacy must work with the Finance department so that the actual cost of the iron dextran is taken into consideration during the charge or price-setting process.

New drug, device, and supply codes should be closely reviewed during the HCPCS Level II update. Just because the HCPCS Level II code is new does not mean that the drug, device, or supply is a recently created item that is new to the marketplace. Perhaps, the drug has been manufactured and administered for several years, but has just now been assigned a HCPCS Level II code. Remember, there are numerous drugs reported under revenue code 025x without a HCPCS Level II code.

HCPCS Level II Update, part 2

In CY 2010, CMS added code J2793 for rilonacept, 1 mg. The CDM team must first determine if this drug is currently utilized by the facility and if so, how is it being charged? Is there a charge item in the CDM for this drug under revenue code 0250 (general pharmacy)? If so, what is the policy and procedure in place for updating this charge item? Do you deactivate the charge item with revenue code 0250 and add a different charge item with revenue code 0636 (drugs requiring detailed code) and code J2793? Do you continue to use the same charge item and simply change revenue code 0250 to 0636 and add code J2793?

Again the CDM team must work with the Pharmacy department to ensure that the new code is included in both the pharmacy order entry system and the CDM with the appropriate data elements and dosage information. If a new charge item was created, the pharmacy order entry staff must be educated so that the correct charge code (charge description number or service code) is ordered when this drug is administered.

Prospective Payment System Updates

The Centers for Medicare and Medicaid (CMS) update their prospective payment systems on a regular schedule throughout the year. Table 3.3 provides a list of the CMS payment systems and their annual update schedule. As you can see, the CMS Inpatient Prospective Payment System (IPPS) is updated on the federal fiscal year with an effective date of October 1. However, the Outpatient Prospective Payment System (OPPS) is updated on the calendar year with an effective date of January 1. Depending on the type of facility or facilities included under the healthcare entity, the CDM coordinator will need to plan for the review of PPS rules and the incorporation of rule changes into the CDM. For example, a CDM coordinator that manages the CDM for the acute care facility as well as the psychiatric unit and the rehabilitation unit will need to be aware of the IPPS, OPPS, Inpatient Rehabilitation Facilities (IRF PPS), and Inpatient Psychiatric Facilities (IPF PPS) rules to ensure a complete and accurate CDM. CMS proposed and final rules are posted on the CMS Web site. Choose the desired payment system area under the Medicare Fee-for-Service Payment section at http://www.cms.hhs.gov/home/medicare.asp.

Program Transmittals

CMS program transmittals are used to communicate new or changed policies, and procedures that are being incorporated into the CMS Manual. Program transmittals will be discussed in more detail in chapter 5, but it is important to include ongoing review of these documents in the CDM maintenance plan.

Table 3.3. CMS payment systems annual update schedule

Service Site	Abbreviation	Relative Weighted Group	Abbreviation	Annual Update
Ambulatory Surgical Center	ASC	Ambulatory Payment Classifications	APCs	January 1
Home Health Agency	HHPPS	Home Health Resource Group	HHRG	October 1
Hospital Outpatient Facility	OPPS	Ambulatory Payment Classifications	APCs	January 1
Inpatient Acute Care Hospital	IPPS	Medicare Severity Diagnosis Related Groups	MS-DRGs	October 1
Inpatient Psychiatric Hospital	IPF PPS	Per diem payment	n/a	July 1
Inpatient Rehabilitation Facility	IRF PPS	Case Mix Group	CMG	October 1
Long Term Care Hospital	LTCH PPS	Medicare Severity Diagnosis Related Groups	MS-DRGs	October 1
Skilled Nursing Facility	SNF PPS	Resource Utilization Group, Version III	RUG III	July 1

CDM coordinators should designate a team member to review program transmittals on a continuous basis. Listservs are available via CMS for specific service areas and are very beneficial because they alert members about significant postings in a timely manner. To join a CMS listserv, visit http://www.cms.hhs.gov/prospmedicarefeesvcpmtgen/downloads/Provider_Listservs.pdf. However, it is a good idea to have this program transmittal review task listed on the maintenance plan to ensure that the review is completed. It is one thing to have documents sent directly to your e-mail account, it is another thing to read the documents and take the action when warranted. In our ever hectic environment it is beneficial to have expectations and reminders in place.

Payer Updates

Although hospitals and other healthcare facilities may prefer to have payer contracts in alignment with their fiscal year, there may be payers that have a set effective period that differs from the facility's fiscal year. Therefore, a schedule of payer contract

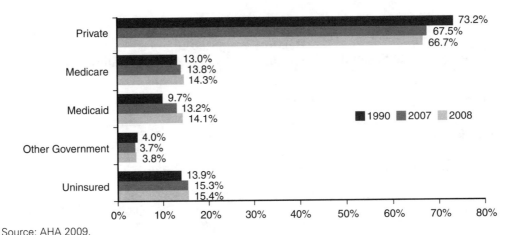

Source: AHA 2009.

Figure 3.1. Distribution of health insurance coverage, percentage of population covered by payer, 1990, 2007, and 2008

updates should be considered in the CDM maintenance plan. The CDM coordinator and payer contract unit must work together to ensure that the CDM reflects billing and coding protocol outlined in the payer contracts.

Many CDM professionals tend to focus on Medicare regulations. However, as you can see from figure 3.1 released by the American Hospital Association, the majority of healthcare services in the United States are provided to patients that have a medical benefit package from a private payer (AHA 2009). Clearly this puts into perspective how important the inclusion of private payer guidelines and requirements are in the CDM maintenance plan.

Policy Alerts

Throughout a payer contract effective period, the payer may send out policy alerts. The policy alerts may contain billing and coding requirements specific to that payer. It is important that the payer contract unit at the facility provide a copy or summary of the policy alerts to the revenue cycle team or CDM unit. Not only may the policy alert require modification to the CDM, it may also warrant changes to order entry as well as education for clinical or ancillary areas.

Compliance Guidance

Compliance guidance is also provided throughout the year. Chapter 5 of this text discusses various compliance documents in detail. However, it is important to provide compliance guidance review tasks on the CDM maintenance plan. Consistent and effective communication between the compliance department and the CDM coordinator is essential.

Other Maintenance

Even with policies, procedures, and maintenance plans in place, there will always be issues that arise and need immediate attention. When issues come to the surface, the CDM coordinator must be ready to execute a CDM review to help identify the root cause of the issue at hand. It is important to address the issue quickly. Not only is reimbursement for rendered services at stake, but the internal cost of claim correct and resubmission can be significant.

Monitoring Rejections and Denials

The CDM coordinator should have constant communication with the claims reconciliation unit. The claims reconciliation unit reviews payer documents to identify if the expected reimbursement matches the actual reimbursement for claims. During data analysis, the reconciliation area may uncover billing, coding, or CDM issues. It is important for the reconciliation, CDM, and coding units to work together to resolve systematic issues.

Human Errors

We are all familiar with the adage "to err is human." Plain and simple, we all make mistakes. Therefore, it is important to make corrections and provide education when human errors are identified. For example, perhaps numeric digits were transposed when they were entered by hand into the CDM as indicated in table 3.4. The internal scrubber did not catch the code transposition error because code 80048 is a valid code. But for the charge item with charge code (that is, service code) 8756214, it is the wrong CPT code. In this case, the CDM review would be conducted immediately so the charge item can be corrected. Not only do the two charge items in question have different charge or price, they also have very different Medicare reimbursement rates. The date of the data entry error should be pinpointed and all claims with charge code 8756214 should be located and corrected. Resubmission of claims may be warranted so that the correct code and charge or price is reported for the service provided to the patient and so that accurate reimbursement can be received.

System Errors in Bill Production or Bill Transmission

Not only may the reconciliation unit uncover human errors, but they may also uncover system errors in claim production and claim transmission. No matter how much system testing the information technology unit provides, there may still be claim production or claim transmission errors. It is important for the CDM coordinator to be aware of and participate in system testing when the CDM is involved. The CDM coordinator may be called upon to communicate the expected outcome for required CDM data elements. For example, it is common for individuals to leave off the leading zero for revenue codes when verbally discussing or informally writing revenue codes. Many say revenue code 360 not 0360. But if the leading zero for revenue codes is left off in data transmission,

Table 3.4. Example of digit transposition

Charge Code 8756214 with Incorrect CPT Code					
Charge Code	Revenue Code	CPT Code	Charge Description	Charge/ Price	Medicare FS Rate 2010
8756214	0300	**80048**	Aldosterone suppression eval panel	$350.00	$12.12
8756849	0300	80048	Basic metabolic panel	$55.00	$12.12
Charge Identifier 8756214 with Correct CPT Code					
Charge Code	Revenue Code	CPT Code	Charge Description	Charge/ Price	Medicare FS Rate
8756214	0300	**80408**	Aldosterone suppression eval panel	$350.00	$179.76
8756849	0300	80048	Basic metabolic panel	$55.00	$12.12

there can be a significant issue. At the payer end, revenue code 360 may be accepted as 3600 instead of 0360. The result is that the line item on the claim is rejected because of the invalid revenue code. Not only will the system issue need to be corrected, but again, all claims containing a 0360 revenue code will need to be reviewed and those where the line item was rejected will need to be adjusted with the payer, as the line item denial or rejection most likely impacted the reimbursement level.

Automation of Chargemaster Maintenance

Not only is CDM maintenance very detail oriented and complicated, it is time consuming. To assist facilities with CDM maintenance, many companies have begun to sell CDM maintenance software packages. Although each maintenance program will have unique and proprietary features, most provide software that will identify revenue codes, CPT/HCPCS codes, and compliance issues for the facility. For example, the program will identify all codes in the client CDM that have been deleted according to the CPT annual update and will provide the facility with replacement choices.

Some of the maintenance programs are installed at the facility and some are provided via the Web. It is important to remember that many of these packages are based on Medicare guidelines although some additionally provide state-level Medicaid regulations. Individual payer regulations are typically not included in these packages, and therefore, specific coding and billing guidance by private payers must be considered and monitored by the facility.

Summary

CDM maintenance is a continual process that must be well designed and monitored by the CDM team. By creating and utilizing a project plan, the CDM coordinator can monitor and report maintenance status to the CDM team as well as Finance and the revenue cycle committee.

References

Acumentra Health. 2005 (December). *Hospital Payment Monitoring Program (HPMP) Compliance Workbook.* Prepared under contract with CMS. http://www.acumentra.org.

American Hospital Association. 2009. Chartbook: Trends Affecting Hospitals and Health Systems, Figure 1.14. http://www.aha.org/aha/research-and-trends/chartbook/ch1.html.

American Medical Association. 2010. CPT® Process—How a Code Becomes a Code. http://www.ama-assn.org/ama/no-index/physician-resources/3882.shtml.

Bielby, Judy A., et al. Care and maintenance of charge masters. *Journal of AHIMA* (Updated March 2010). http://library.ahima.org/xpedio/groups/public/document/ahima/bok1_047258.hcsp?dDocName=bok1_04728.

Casto, A. and E. Layman. 2010. *Principles of Healthcare Reimbursement.* Chicago: AHIMA.

Dietz, M. S. 2005 (October). Ensure equitable reimbursement through an accurate charge description master. *Proceedings from AHIMA's 77th National Convention and Exhibit.* Chicago: AHIMA.

Harman, L. 2006. *Ethical Challenges in the Management of Health Information.* Sudbury, MA: Jones and Bartlett. 11, 113.

Resources

Drach, M., A. Davis, and C. Sagrati. 2001. Ten steps to successful chargemaster reviews. *Journal of AHIMA* 72(1):42–48.

Healthcare Financial Management Association. Summer 2003 Patient Friendly Billing Report. http://www.hfma.org/HFMA-Initiatives/Patient-Friendly-Billing/Patient-Friendly-Billing-Project-Reports/.

Leeds, E. 2001 (October). When good chargemasters go bad. *Proceedings from AHIMA's 73rd National Convention and Exhibit.* Chicago: AHIMA.

Richey, J. 2001. A new approach to chargemaster management. *Journal of AHIMA* 72(1):51–55.

Chapter 4

Managing CDM Workflow

Anne B. Casto, RHIA, CCS

CDM Workflow

Workflow is essentially the process of passing information, tasks, or documents from one employee or work area to another until the final product is produced. The coordination of the process or processes is workflow management. The concept is very similar to revenue cycle and revenue cycle management discussed in chapter 1. Some benefits of using workflow and workflow management are:

- Unnecessary steps are eliminated
- Responsibilities are documented
- Performance is easily tracked
- Methods are standardized, resulting in a consistent product

There are numerous workflow models and software packages available for healthcare facilities to utilize. Just search "workflow management" on the Internet and over four million links are returned. Your healthcare organization may have already adopted a particular workflow management style or workflow management software package. CDM coordinators that are designing workflows for CDM management should discuss workflow software options with the IT management team to maintain consistency throughout the organization.

As discussed in chapter 1, organization and execution of established processes are paramount to a complete and accurate CDM. What makes workflows a little tricky is that there is no one way to maintain the CDM. Each facility is different, and therefore, each facility will establish a customized workflow(s) for CDM management to meet their internal needs. This chapter will discuss key components of the CDM workflow and provide focus points for CDM teams to consider when designing and executing CDM workflows.

Workflow Participants

Which departments are included in the workflow will depend on the structure of the healthcare facility. Typically, the following departments or areas are part of the revenue cycle team and therefore take part in CDM maintenance:

- Finance
- Patient accounting
- Ancillary departments
- Information systems or technology
- Health information management
- Compliance
- Legal (Dietz 2005)

Each member of the revenue cycle team will have a different role in CDM maintenance. Some participants will compile data, review reports, and gather data while others will review the information and provide feedback based on their expertise. Others will review information and discuss the impact that CDM changes will have on their area. However, understanding how changes will impact the revenue cycle before the change is executed will help the CDM team make informed decisions and will also help to prevent undesirable events from taking place.

Designing Workflows

Workflows should be developed based on positions in the facility, not individual persons. In this section, three workflows are discussed: adding a charge item, modifying a charge item, and deleting or deactivating a charge item. Please keep in mind that this is just one model. You may choose to expand on these basic workflows based on your facility's needs. The workflows are intended to give the CDM team guidance when a change is requested from an area outside of the CDM unit. Similar workflows could be developed for annual CPT/HCPCS code updates.

Adding Charge Items

New charge items will need to be added to the CDM. Your facility's service offering will change based on community needs. Additionally, a clinical or ancillary department may purchase new equipment that allows new services to be performed; this too would warrant new charge items to be added to the CDM. When this situation arises, the CDM team should execute the workflow for the addition of a new charge item.

Considerations

In this case, all data elements for the charge item must be determined. The CDM team may need to benchmark best practices in reporting if this is a new service for which the CDM team is unfamiliar. The Finance department must be alerted to begin the process for establishing a new charge or price. The finance team may require lead time to benchmark comparative pricing data in order to establish a charge or price that is right for the facility's market.

Figure 4.1 provides a sample workflow for the addition of a charge item to the CDM. Note there are an increased number of tasks at the beginning of this workflow. When a new line item is requested, the proper research must take place to ensure that the line item is complete, accurate, and compliant.

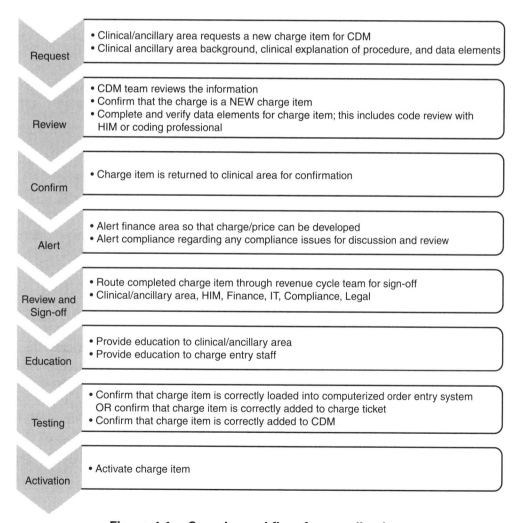

Request
- Clinical/ancillary area requests a new charge item for CDM
- Clinical ancillary area background, clinical explanation of procedure, and data elements

Review
- CDM team reviews the information
- Confirm that the charge is a NEW charge item
- Complete and verify data elements for charge item; this includes code review with HIM or coding professional

Confirm
- Charge item is returned to clinical area for confirmation

Alert
- Alert finance area so that charge/price can be developed
- Alert compliance regarding any compliance issues for discussion and review

Review and Sign-off
- Route completed charge item through revenue cycle team for sign-off
- Clinical/ancillary area, HIM, Finance, IT, Compliance, Legal

Education
- Provide education to clinical/ancillary area
- Provide education to charge entry staff

Testing
- Confirm that charge item is correctly loaded into computerized order entry system OR confirm that charge item is correctly added to charge ticket
- Confirm that charge item is correctly added to CDM

Activation
- Activate charge item

Figure 4.1. Sample workflow for new line item

Modifying Charge Items

At some point a charge item will need to be revised. The CDM team should have a protocol in place for instances when a clinical area approaches the CDM team for a change (Bielby, et al. 2010). When this situation arises, the CDM team should execute the workflow for the modification of a charge item.

Considerations

Even though only one data element may be revised, it is a good time to consider if all other data elements are up to date. Does changing the CPT code require a revenue code change or a charge description change? The CDM coordinator should also consider how the modification to this charge item may impact the completeness of the CDM. If the charge item in question is modified, does this result in the need for an additional line charge to be added as well? The Finance department should be alerted to discuss if the charge or price should be adjusted. Be ready to discuss changes in OPPS relative weight with the finance team if there is a change to the CPT/HCPCS code.

Figure 4.2 provides a sample workflow for modifying a charge item in the CDM. Again, this is a basic workflow. Your facility may want to expand upon this workflow based on your facility's needs.

Deleting or Deactivating Charge Items

Whether charge items are deleted or deactivated will depend on the facility's philosophy for CDM maintenance. Nonetheless, there will be an instance when a charge item needs to be deleted or deactivated. Perhaps the facility has decided to close the pain management clinic or the wound care clinic. When this situation arises, the CDM team should execute the workflow for the deletion or deactivation of a charge item.

Considerations

Before a charge item is deleted or deactivated, there are several angles to examine. Is the service in question performed by any other clinical or ancillary area in the healthcare facility? Perhaps by an off-campus or another on-campus area that shares the main CDM? The CDM team should add a task for the production and review of a charge item charge history in the workflow. The charge item charge history and utilization reports will assist the CDM coordinator in determining which area has utilized the charge item under consideration for deletion or deactivation. If the charge item is utilized by more than one service area or facility, input from the impacted areas will need to be gathered and considered during the workflow.

Also, the CDM team should consider what other charge items are most often activated along with the charge item in question. Should other charge items be deleted

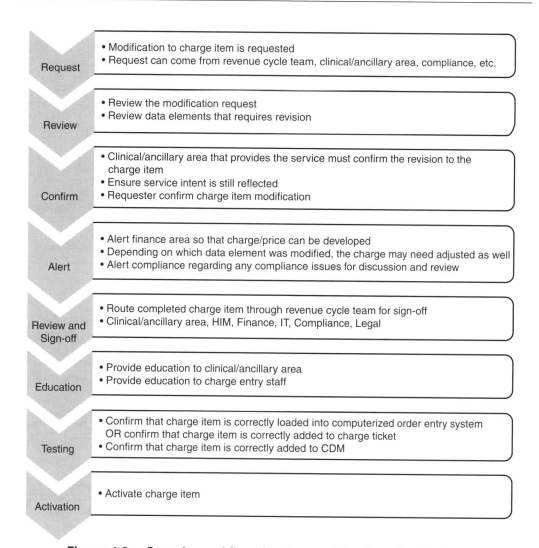

Figure 4.2.   Sample workflow for the modification of a line item

or deactivated as well? Include the production and review of a resource consumption report to the workflow. The resource consumption report will allow the CDM team to identify charge items that are most often activated along with the charge item in question. Analysis of the resource consumption report will assist the CDM team with identifying charge items that may also require deletion or deactivation or modification.

Figure 4.3 provides a sample workflow for the deletion or deactivation of a charge item from the CDM. Again, there is a considerable amount of research that should be performed prior to the deletion or deactivation of the charge item.

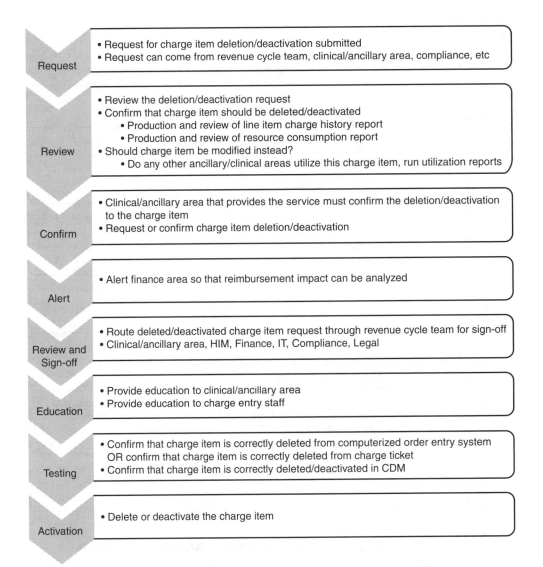

Figure 4.3. **Sample workflow for deleted or deactivated line item**

Adding New Departments

New clinical or ancillary areas may be added to the healthcare facility. Additionally, areas that have traditionally been soft-coded (HIM coded) areas, such as cardiac catheterization lab or gastrointestinal services lab, may want to move to a hard-coded system. In these situations, multiple charge items will need to be added to the CDM. In this instance, the CDM team should execute the workflow for the addition of a new department to the CDM. The workflow for adding charge items to the CDM can be used for this project. However, it is very important for the CDM team to fully understand the service offerings so that all required charge items can be added to the CDM prior to the go-live date for the delivery of services.

Considerations

The CDM team should interview the ancillary or clinical department in order to identify all the services that will be provided, all the billable supplies that will be utilized, and the possible drugs for administration. The CDM team will then need to decipher which services, supplies, or drugs are already included in the CDM and which items will need to have a new charge item created. This is a very important process to ensure that duplicate charge items are not added to the CDM. Additionally, the Finance department will require adequate time to research and benchmark comparative pricing data prior to the activation of the charge items for a new department.

For those departments that are moving from soft-coding to hard-coding, an interview process is also warranted. It is important for the CDM team to be fully aware of how each charge is currently captured. The CDM team will then need to ensure that all charges continue to be captured under the hard-coded format. The CDM team may even uncover areas of missed charges during this process. It is very important for the CDM team to have good communication with the coding unit regarding the transition date. If the coding unit continues to soft-code encounters past the transition date, duplicate charges may appear on the patient's account and result in overpayment by the payer.

Monitoring the Workflow

The CDM coordinator will need to manage the workflow to ensure that assigned tasks are completed in a timely manner. This is no easy task considering that multiple workflows may be in progress at the same time. If your facility utilizes workflow management software, then most likely the software will provide a tracking mechanism that the CDM coordinator can use to manage the CDM processes. However, if your facility is not using a pre-designed workflow package, then the CDM coordinator should consider designing a workflow tracking system to manage this very complicated process.

Documentation

The workflow tasks and activities should be documented. Again, if your facility utilizes workflow management software, it most likely includes a documentation component. However, if you do not use a software package at your facility, the CDM coordinator must ensure that all CDM workflow activities are documented. Note that there was a research component in the workflows previously discussed. If your CDM team fails to properly document workflow activities as they are completed, it will make the research required in the future very difficult.

Communicating Changes

A critical task for all CDM maintenance workflows is the communication of the CDM change. Whether it is a modification, addition, or deletion or deactivation of a charge item, the change must be communicated to the affected areas.

Update Computerized Physician Order Entry System (CPOE)

Modifications of the CDM should carry through to modifications in the computerized physician order entry system (CPOE). The CDM team should work with IT to ensure that the charge requirements are properly crafted. The CDM team should be involved in system testing to ensure that the changes made to the CPOE system are accurate.

Update Charge Tickets

If charge tickets (superbills) are utilized, then copies of the old charge tickets must be replaced with the new charge tickets. This may not be as easy as it seems. Employees may keep a charge ticket supply in their desk drawer, or they may have the electronic document saved in a personal folder on the computer. Using outdated versions of a charge ticket can result in missed charges or inaccurate charge data being submitted on the patient claim. The CDM team should have a procedure in place to ensure that the changes to charge tickets are properly executed each time a change is warranted.

Education

Education should be provided when changes are made to the CDM. The education may be provided for the entire revenue cycle team, or may be tailored for a specific clinical or ancillary department or unit. When a new charge item(s) or new department is added, the CDM-significant education should be provided to the impacted areas. Alerts should be provided to order entry areas so that the order entry staff members are aware that a change has been made and how they are impacted. For example, when a physician goes to the computerized order entry system and cannot locate the charge he or she typically activates, what will he or she do? At times, the CDM team may need to be creative in their education tactics. Some healthcare professionals may find the revenue cycle and CDM to be a "dry" topic. In this instance, the CDM team must strive to engage the audience and help them to understand the important facts and issues so that the healthcare facility can remain compliant and financially stable with the production of accurate and complete claims.

References

Bielby, Judy A., et al. Care and maintenance of charge masters. *Journal of AHIMA* (Updated March 2010). http://library.ahima.org/xpedio/groups/public/document/ahima/bok1_047258. hcsp?dDocName=bok1_04728.

Dietz, M. S. 2005 (October). Ensure equitable reimbursement through an accurate charge description master. *Proceedings from AHIMA's 77th National Convention and Exhibit.* Chicago: AHIMA.

Resources

Leeds, E. 2001 (October). When good chargemasters go bad. *Proceedings from AHIMA's 73rd National Convention and Exhibit.* Chicago: AHIMA.

Richey, J. 2001. A new approach to chargemaster management. *Journal of AHIMA* 72(1):51–55.

Stone, F., J. Egan, R. LeBoutillier, and D. Blackwelder. 2006 (October). Opening Pandora's box: Pure coding vs. charge master driven coding—a case study at Duke University health system. *Proceedings from AHIMA's 78th National Convention and Exhibit.* Chicago: AHIMA.

Chapter 5

The Relationship between Charge Description Master and Compliance

**Erica Leeds, MIS, RHIA, CCS, CCS-P,
and Anne B. Casto, RHIA, CCS**

In today's healthcare environment every facility has a compliance plan. It is important for the CDM unit's policies and procedures to be in alignment with the facility's compliance plan. Since coding and billing impact reimbursement, it is a highly regulated area (Bowman 2008, 115). The CDM unit must pay close attention and develop protocol to ensure compliance with the laws, regulations, and requirements for all payers, both government and private. It is definitely a challenge to stay up to date with all the compliance guidance. Making compliance guidance a part of regular activities in the CDM maintenance plan will help ensure that the CDM team stays focused on compliance. Likewise, a good working relationship with the facility's compliance department will help the CDM team address and resolve difficult compliance issues.

Compliance Guidance

There are numerous publications and policy documents that must be reviewed and assessed throughout the year in order to keep the CDM compliant with coding and billing regulations. This chapter provides an overview of many publications that impact CDM maintenance. Though many of these documents pertain to Medicare, private payer regulations should not be forgotten. Although numerous private payers have adopted compliance guidelines similar to Medicare, the specifics for each payer should be closely examined and incorporated into the facility's CDM.

Medicare Claims Processing Manual

The CMS Claims Processing Manual (Publication number 100-04) is one of the many manuals included in CMS Internet-Only Manuals System. The Internet-Only Manuals System is used by CMS program components, partners, contracts, and other agencies to administer CMS programs. Day-to-day operating instructions, policies and procedures based on statutes, regulations, guidelines, models, and directives are included in the manuals (CMS 2010a). Though three manuals are still provided in hard copy, the majority of manuals were converted to a Web-based, user-friendly system in 2003. The manuals can be found at http://www.cms.hhs.gov/Manuals/IOM/list.asp. Figure 5.1 shows a snippet from the CMS Internet-Only Manuals (IOM) Web page.

The Medicare Claims Processing Manual currently has 38 chapters and provides guidance for producing claims for all healthcare settings (inpatient, outpatient rehabilitation, and the like). General billing requirements as well as service area-specific requirements are provided. A CDM coordinator may need to be familiar with many of the chapters, and he or she may study more closely the requirements outlined for the service areas included in their hospital's own book of business. For example, the CDM coordinator may have a cursory understanding of Ambulatory Surgical Center regulations, but may have a detailed understanding of hospital inpatient requirements.

Updates to the Medicare Claims Processing Manual are made throughout the year based on changes made to the unique prospective payment systems. For example, changes brought about by the final IPPS rule in August would be incorporated in the Medicare Claims Processing Manual by October 1. However, the modifications from the final OPPS rule in November would be incorporated by January 1. One great feature is that CMS displays changes to the Claims Processing Manual in red. Therefore, the CDM Coordinator can browse the individual chapter and easily locate recent changes.

Publication #	Title
100	Introduction
100-01	Medicare General Information, Eligibility, and Entitlement Manual
100-02	Medicare Benefit Policy Manual
100-03	**Medicare National Coverage Determinations (NCD) Manual**
100-04	**Medicare Claims Processing Manual**
100-05	Medicare Secondary Payer Manual
100-06	Medicare Financial Management Manual
100-07	State Operations Manual
100-08	**Medicare Program Integrity Manual**
100-09	Medicare Contractor Beneficiary and Provider Communications Manual

Source: CMS 2010a.
*Manuals highlighted in this figure are the manuals that are discussed in detail in Chapter 5 of this text.

Figure 5.1.   CMS Internet-Only Manuals (IOM) Web page

CMS Program Transmittals

Program Transmittals are used by CMS to communicate policies and procedures for the specific prospective payment systems' program manuals. Current and historic transmittals dating back to 2000 can be found on the CMS Web site at http://www.cms. hhs.gov/transmittals/01_overview.asp (CMS 2005). Figure 5.2 shows the anatomy of a typical transmittal.

As discussed in Chapter 3, CDM Professionals should stay up to date with program transmittals released for Part A and Part B Medicare payment systems. The transmittals should be read carefully and the information should be communicated effectively to the compliance department, revenue cycle team, and CDM team. Any issues related to the CDM should be incorporated into the facility's active CDM as warranted. The CDM coordinator should keep an audit trail of changes made to the CDM based on program transmittal guidance.

National and Local Coverage Determinations

National Coverage Determinations (NCDs) describe the circumstances under which specific medical supplies, services, or procedures are covered nationwide by Medicare under title XVIII of the Social Security Act and other Medical regulations and ruling. Once the NCD has been published, it is binding for all Medicare contractors (Medicare Administrative Contracts (MACs), Durable Medical Equipment Regional Contractors (DMERCS), Quality Improvement Organizations (QIOs), Program Safeguard

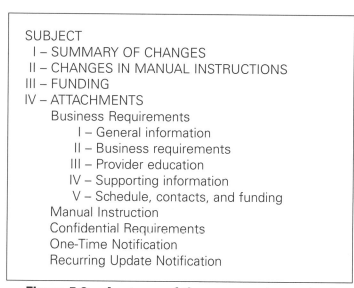

```
SUBJECT
  I – SUMMARY OF CHANGES
  II – CHANGES IN MANUAL INSTRUCTIONS
  III – FUNDING
  IV – ATTACHMENTS
        Business Requirements
            I – General information
            II – Business requirements
            III – Provider education
            IV – Supporting information
            V – Schedule, contacts, and funding
        Manual Instruction
        Confidential Requirements
        One-Time Notification
        Recurring Update Notification
```

Figure 5.2. Anatomy of the program transmittal

Contractors (PSCs), and so on) (CMS 2008). Additionally, contractors are responsible for notifying the provider community of an NCD release. Contractors do not have the authority to deviate from an NCD when absolute words such as "never" or "only if" are used in the policy. When reviewing coverage issues, the contractors may cover services at their own discretion based on a local coverage determination if an NCD is not established (CMS 2008).

Local Coverage Determinations (LCDs), formerly Local Medical Review Policies or LMRPs, provide facilities and physicians with the circumstances under which a service, procedure, or supply is considered medically necessary. An LCD is used to determine coverage on a Medicare Administrative Contractor-wide, intermediary-wide, or carrier-wide basis (rather than nationwide like an NCD). There are regional differences in medical necessity and therefore differences in coverage for Medicare supplies, services, and procedures (CMS 2008). LCDs are educational materials intended to assist facilities and providers with correct billing and claim processing. Within the LCD is a listing of ICD-9-CM codes that indicate what is covered and what is not covered. Additionally, there may be a listing of the HCPCS codes for which the LCD applies.

It is important to understand the difference between coverage and medical necessity. For example, chest x-rays are covered by Medicare. However, the service is only reimbursed by Medicare when it is deemed medically necessary. This means that the physician has to provide sufficient medical documentation, through ICD-9-CM diagnosis coding, to substantiate that the service is warranted for diagnostic or therapeutic treatment of the patient. Medicare does not pay for services that are not medically necessary.

The Medicare National Coverage Determinations Manual (NCD) is one of the Internet-Only Manuals (IOMs) published by CMS. This manual provides a listing of all topics included in the numerous active NCDs. The publication number for the NCD manual is 100-03 (see figure 5.1.)

The NCD manual consists of two chapters: 1 – Coverage Determinations and 2 – HCPCS Codes for Services Described in National Coverage Determinations Manual. However, only chapter one, Coverage Determinations Parts 1–4, is ready for use by providers. Chapter one provides listing of all NCDs currently in effect. Figure 5.3 provides a sample of current NCDs.

In order to gain a clear understanding of coverage issues, let us examine NCD 140.2, which is shown in Figure 5.4. From the information provided in this NCD it is clear that Medicare Program payment will not be made for breast reconstruction for cosmetic reasons. Cosmetic surgery is excluded from coverage under §1862(a)(10) of the Act. However, breast reconstruction following the removal of a breast for any medical

140 - Miscellaneous Surgical Procedures
140.1 - Abortion
140.2 - Breast Reconstruction Following Mastectomy
140.3 - Transsexual Surgery
140.4 - Plastic Surgery to Correct "Moon Face"
140.5 - Laser Procedures

Figure 5.3.   Sample of current NCDs

140.2 - Breast reconstruction following mastectomy

(Rev. 1, 10-03-03)

CIM 35-47

During recent years, there has been a considerable change in the treatment of diseases of the breast such as fibrocystic disease and cancer. While extirpation of the disease remains of primary importance, the quality of life following initial treatment is increasingly recognized as of great concern. The increased use of breast reconstruction procedures is due to several factors:

- A change in epidemiology of breast cancer, including an apparent increase in incidence;
- Improved surgical skills and techniques;
- The continuing development of better prostheses; and
- Increasing awareness by physicians of the importance of postsurgical psychological adjustment.

Reconstruction of the affected and the contralateral unaffected breast following a medically necessary mastectomy is considered a relatively safe and effective non-cosmetic procedure. Accordingly, program payment may be made for breast reconstruction surgery following removal of a breast for any medical reason.

Source: CMS 2010b

Figure 5.4.   NCD 140.2 – Breast Reconstruction Following Mastectomy

reason is a covered procedure. This coverage determination applies to both the affected and the contralateral unaffected breast (CMS 2010b).

Additional information regarding LCDs can be located in the Medicare Program Integrity Manual (Publication number 100-08), Chapter 13, Local Coverage Determinations. Chapter 13 outlines Medicare policy regarding NCDs and LCDs and then provides the regulations for LCD creation, modification, distribution, execution, and appeals.

When examining LCDs it is important to understand the difference between policies and articles. An LCD policy contains only the reasonable and necessary provision regarding the supply, procedure, or service. For example, a list of codes describing which conditions provide for medical necessity and which conditions do not warrant medical necessity may be provided in a LCD policy.

An article is used by the Medicare Administrative Contractor (MAC) to provide guidelines about the benefit category, statutory exclusions, and coding provisions. For example, coding guidelines relating to diagnosis codes in the medical necessity code list would be provided in an article, not in the LCD policy itself. Therefore, in order to fully understand an LCD and effectively implement it, a CDM professional must read the policy as well as any associated articles.

To find NCDs and LCDs for a specific geographical area, CDM professionals can access the Medicare Coverage Database at http://www.cms.hhs.gov/mcd/search.asp. This search engine allows the user to search documents of national coverage or local coverage. Additionally, the user can search articles and policies by geographic area or MAC. It also allows for the user to enter search criteria, such as CPT/HCPCS code, keywords, ICD-9-CM codes, coverage topics, and date criteria.

National Correct Coding Initiative

National Correct Coding Initiative (NCCI) edits have been in place for outpatient claim editing since January 1, 1996. There are two sets of NCCI edits, one for the physician setting and one for the hospital outpatient setting. The hospital outpatient setting edits are embedded in the integrated outpatient code editor (IOCE) used by Medicare Administrative Contractors (MACs) to process claims under OPPS.

The purpose of the NCCI edits is to ensure proper CPT and HCPCS coding for Medicare Part B services. This set of edits are not medical necessity denial edits, rather they are in place to ensure correct coding and payment. The edits are designed to audit CPT codes based on the CPT coding conventions, national and local policies and edits, coding guidelines developed by national societies, analysis of standard medical and surgical practices, and a review of current coding practices (CMS 2010c).

Within the set of edits, there are two types: comprehensive code edits and mutually exclusive code edits. The comprehensive code edits are designed to identify instances where the most comprehensive code was not reported, but rather components of that service were reported or when a comprehensive code and a component code are reported together. Reporting component codes rather than a comprehensive code is against coding guidelines and could lead to overpayment. This set of edits ensures that

CPT code 80061 (lipid panel) includes the following tests:

CPT code 82465 – Cholesterol, serum or whole blood, total
CPT code 83718 – Lipoprotein, direct; HDL cholesterol
CPT code 84478 – Triglycerides

When all these tests are performed, the panel test, CPT code 80061, should be reported in place of the individual tests.

Source: CMS 2010c.

Figure 5.5.   NCCI comprehensive code edit

Free skin grafts are coded by type (partial or full), location, and size. Only one type of skin graft is typically applied for a specific area. Therefore, free skin graft CPT codes 15100, 15120, 15200, 15220, 15240, and 15260 are mutually exclusive to one another. Therefore, the following codes are mutually exclusive and should not be reported together for the same body area – trunk:

CPT code 15100 – split thickness autograft, trunk, arms, legs; first 100 sq cm or less, or one percent of body area of infants and children

CPT code 15200 – full thickness graft, free, including direct closure of donor site, trunk; 20 sq. cm or less

The medical record and operative report should be closely reviewed to determine which type of free skin graft was utilized.

Source: CMS 2010c.

Figure 5.6.   NCCI mutually exclusive code edit

only the comprehensive code will receive payment. Figure 5.5 provides an example of a comprehensive code edit.

Additionally, the NCCI contains mutually exclusive edits. These code combinations consist of codes that would not reasonably be reported together or should not be reported together. Figure 5.6 provides an example of a NCCI mutually exclusive edit.

Claims violating NCCI edits will receive the following messages on Medicare correspondence as indicated in figure 5.7. Remember that the Medicare Summary Notice is provided to the patient and the Remittance Notice is issued to the facility.

CMS publishes the National Correct Coding Initiative Policy Manual for Medicare Services, which can be obtained from the CMS Web site. Additionally, the Medicare Claims Processing Manual contains information regarding the NCCI edits in Chapter

---

Medicare Summary Notice (MSN)

    Message 16.8 - Payment is included in another service received on the same day

    Message 16.9 - This allowance has been reduced by the amount previously paid for a related procedure

Remittance Notice Messages

    Claim adjustment reason code 97 – **The benefit for this service is included in the payment/allowance for another service/procedure that has already been adjudicated.**

    Claim adjustment reason code 231 – **Mutually exclusive procedures cannot be done in the same day/setting**

    Remark code M80 – **Not covered when performed during the same session/ date as a previously processed service for the patient**

Source: CMS 2010d; **Washington Publishing Company 2010.**

Figure 5.7.   NCCI rejection/denial messages

23, Section 20.9. Chapter 23, Section 20.9.1, Correct Coding Modifier Indicators and HCPCS Codes Modifiers, discusses the NCCI edits that allow for modifiers to be used by providers to indicate special circumstances when the code edit should be bypassed based on the patient's specific course of treatment (CMS 2009). Table 5.1 provides a list of the approved CPT and HCPCS Level II modifiers that are not subject to CCI edits. Several modifiers have specific usage guidelines to prevent fraud and abuse situations. For example, instructional articles have been published regarding modifier 59.

Integrated Outpatient Code Editor

The Medicare Integrated Outpatient Code Editor (IOCE) is a software program designed to process data for OPPS pricing and to audit facility claims data. The processing function prepares submitted claims data for the Medicare Pricer by:

- Assigning the appropriate Ambulatory Payment Classifications (APCs)
- Assigning the CMS-designated status indicators
- Computing discounts, if applicable
- Determining a claim disposition based on generated edits
- Determining if packaging is applicable
- Determining payment adjustments, if applicable (3M 2010, 1.6)

The editing function audits claims for coding and data entry errors. The extensive edits in the IOCE are applied to claims, individual diagnoses and procedures, and code sets.

Table 5.1. Approved CPT and HCPCS Level II modifiers not subject to CCI edits

Modifier(s)	Modifier description
E1–E4	Eyelids
FA and F1–F9	Left and right hand digits
TA and T1–T9	Left and right foot digits
LT	Left side
RT	Right side
25	Significant, separately identifiable evaluation and management service by the same physician on the same day of the procedure or other service
58	Staged or related procedure or service by the same physician during the postoperative period
59	Distinct procedural service
78	Unplanned return to the Operating Room following initial procedure for a related procedure during the postoperative period
79	Unrelated procedure or service by the same physician during the postoperative period
LC	Left circumflex, coronary artery
LD	Left anterior descending coronary artery
RC	Right coronary artery
91	Repeat clinical diagnostic laboratory test

Source: CMS 2009.

Table 5.2 provides a sample of edits included in the IOCE. When activated, IOCE edits have an associated line or claim disposition attached to them. Table 5.3 provides a listing of the edit dispositions and their definitions.

Depending on the claim disposition, providers or facilities may correct the claim or process write-offs based on facility policy. It is critical for facilities to monitor and analyze claim disposition composition. Possible reasons for claim errors should be investigated, and corrective action should be taken when applicable. Most revenue cycle teams have an ongoing quality monitoring process in place so that resolutions to claim errors can be incorporated into the process.

For example, in January the reconciliation unit at Hospital A begins to see Medicare bills with rejections for IOC edit #48, revenue center requires HCPCS. Upon investigation it is found that a line item for a newly added CPT code is missing the CPT code in the CDM. Therefore, when the charge identifier is sent to the patient's account, the revenue code is sent, but the CPT code is not. Perhaps during the annual update, the

Table 5.2.   Sample of the edits included in the OCE

Edit	Generated when....
1. Invalid diagnosis code	The principal diagnosis field is blank, there are no diagnoses entered on the claim, or the entered diagnosis code is not valid for the selected version of the program.
2. Diagnosis and age conflict	The diagnosis code includes an age range, and the age is outside that range.
8. Procedure and sex conflict	The procedure code includes sex designation, and the sex does not match.
19. Mutually exclusive procedure that is not allowed by NCCI even if appropriate modifier is present	The procedure is one of a pair of mutually exclusive procedures in the NCCI table coded on the same day, where the use of a modifier is not appropriate. Only the code in column 2 of a mutually exclusive pair is rejected; the column 1 code of the pair is not marked as an edit.
20. Code 2 of a code pair that is not allowed by NCCI even if appropriate modifier is present	The procedure is identified as part of another procedure on the claim coded on the same day, where the use of a modifier is not appropriate. Only the code in column 2 of a code pair is rejected; the column 1 code of the pair is not marked as an edit.
28. Code not recognized by Medicare; alternate code for same service may be available	The procedure code has a "Not recognized by Medicare" indicator.
41. Invalid revenue code	The revenue code is not in the list of valid revenue code entries.
43. Transfusion or blood product exchange without specification of blood product	A blood transfusion or exchange is coded but no blood product is coded.
71. Claim lacks required device code	The code for a device designated as necessary for an outpatient procedure coded on the claim is missing. This edit is bypassed when the modifier is 52, 73, or 74.

Source: 3M Health Information System 2010.

Table 5.3. Listing of the edit dispositions and their definitions

Disposition	Definition
Claim rejection	The provider can correct and resubmit the claim but cannot appeal the rejection
	Currently not assigned to edits
Claim denial	The provider cannot resubmit the claim but can appeal the denial
	Example: Edit 27 – Only incidental services reported (all line items are bundled services under HOPPS)
Claim return to provider (RTP)	The provider can resubmit the claim once the problems are corrected
	Example: Edit 1 – Invalid diagnosis code
Claim suspension	The claim is not returned to the provider, but it is not processed for payment until the fiscal intermediary (FI) makes a determination or obtains further information
	Example: Edit 12 – Questionable covered service
Line item rejection	The claim can be processed for payment with some line items rejected for payment (i.e., the line item can be corrected and resubmitted but cannot be appealed)
	Example: Edit 19 – Mutually exclusive procedure that is not allowed by NCCI even if appropriate modifier is present
Line item denial	There are one or more edits that cause one or more individual line items to be denied. The claim can be processed for payment with some line items denied for payment (i.e., the line item cannot be resubmitted but can be appealed)
	Example: Edit 9 – Non-covered for reasons other than statute

Source: 3M Health Information System 2010.

line item was created, but the CPT code was not entered into the line item. Though this is somewhat of a simple fix to the CDM—the CPT code is added to the line item—it is a wake-up call to the CDM unit that quality review of the CDM annual update may need to be revisited and the process improved.

Device-Procedure/Procedure-Device Edits

CMS utilized historical claims data to set reimbursement rates for services under OPPS. In order to set accurate and representative rates, the claims data for a given service must be complete. Because supplies are most often packaged under OPPS, CMS implemented the device-procedure/procedure-device edits to ensure that facilities would report both the supply charge item and the procedure charge item for device-

Device	Device Description	Procedure	Procedure Description	Effective Date	Implementation Date	Termination Date
C1721	AICD, dual chamber	33224	Insert pacing lead	1/1/2007	1/1/2007	
C1721	AICD, dual chamber	33240	Insert pulse generator	1/1/2008	1/1/2008	
C1721	AICD, dual chamber	33249	Insert electro lead	1/1/2008	1/1/2008	
C1721	AICD, dual chamber	G0298	Insert dual chamber/cd	1/1/2007	1/1/2007	12/31/2007
C1721	AICD, dual chamber	G0300	Insert reposit lead dual+gen	1/1/2007	1/1/2007	12/31/2007

Source: CMS 2010e.

Figure 5.8. Sample device-procedure edit

dependent surgical procedures. These sets of edits are included in the IOCE (edits #71 and #77)(CMS 2010e). Figure 5.8 provides a sample device-procedure edit.

The edits are updated quarterly and posted on the CMS Web site at http://www.cms. hhs.gov/HospitalOutpatientPPS/02_device_procedure.asp#TopOfPage. CDM professionals should review the edits annually to ensure that all devices used by the facility have line item charges with the correct HCPCS Level II supply code included in the CDM. CDM professionals must also confirm that the line item charge is also included in the order entry system and, in addition, provide education to charge entry staff.

Payer Specific Edits

Payer specific edits must also be taken into consideration by the compliance department and the CDM team. For example, the state workers compensation (WC) may not cover preventive immunizations. However, they may cover tetanus shots post injury and have advised facilities to report these charges in revenue code 0450 via a policy alert. The claims processing system at the WC contains an edit to deny claim line items reported with revenue codes 0770–0779, preventive care services. Therefore, when a tetanus administration is provided to a WC patient in the emergency department, the code would need to be reported with revenue code 0450 rather than 0771 for that specific payer.

Determining Compliance

You have incorporated compliance into your CDM policies and procedures; you have added compliance review tasks into the CDM maintenance plan. So how do you know your CDM is compliant? Monitoring and auditing are key sections of the facility's overall compliance plan. Auditing, both internal and external, is discussed in detail in Chapter 7 of this text. Coding is a highly monitored and audited area for most healthcare facilities. Therefore, the CDM unit should work with the HIM department to ensure that both hard-coded and soft-coded procedures are included in monitoring and auditing plans.

Likewise, the CDM unit should work with the compliance department to ensure the validation of hard-coded services is included in audits performed for specific clinical areas. For example, your compliance department has arranged for an outside firm to review radiation therapy services. Some of the radiation oncology procedures are soft-coded and some are hard-coded in the CDM. The CDM unit should request to be involved in the audit proceeding. The CDM coordinator should be present at the audit pre- and post-review sessions with the outside firm. It is important for the CDM coordinator to understand the structure of the audit as well as the outcomes so that corrective action can be taken where warranted.

CDM units should have an annual calendar of monitoring and auditing events. Regular monitoring of high risk or problem areas will help the CDM unit identify issues early on and hopefully will mitigate error claims, or at least help to reduce the impact of compliance issues.

Communicating Compliance

To have an effective communication plan for identifying, resolving, and correcting compliance issues within the CDM, you must have a strong team of various skill sets. Ideally, your facility would create a team to address compliance issues. The team should include:

- Person responsible for the maintenance of the charge description master
- Representation or skill set from the Compliance department
- Representation or skill set from the Coding department
- Representation or skill set from the Patient Accounting department
- Representation or skill set from the Denials department
- Representation or skill set from the Auditing department
- Representation or skill set from the ancillary departments
- Sponsorship from a member of upper management

Depending on the size of your hospital, a representative could wear more than one hat or, rather, have shared responsibilities for each of these departments. A smaller hospital could have one HIM manager responsible for compliance, coding, and auditing, whereas a larger hospital could have a manager, supervisor, and team lead for each of these departments. The key to a successful team is having the right people, with the right attitude, and with the right skill set. Then you must have sponsorship from leaders that are willing to help you take the necessary steps to correct the situation—even if those steps are not always popular with the ancillary departments, as they will cause extra steps in their processes. This process must always balance the workload among the departments in order to be an effective program for the hospital.

Each hospital has a set of staff members that are more passionate about charging and billing than others. The ideal situation is to rely on those staff members for your compliance team. However, you may not have those unique individuals from which to draw expertise, and you may have to develop a team that has a healthy respect for the task of keeping hospitals compliant. If you have a team member that is less than enthusiastic about being on the team and is not contributing in a positive manner, then your ability to impact change can be stalled or halted.

Type and Form of Communication

Once you have established a compliance team, then the team needs to agree on what types of compliance guidance and issues will be communicated. Likewise, the team will need to determine how or what form of communication is best.

Types of Communication

There are several different ways to communicate compliance guidance and issues to the appropriate areas in the healthcare facility. Some types of communication that your CDM team may want to consider are:

- Updates from the regulations, edits, or policies
- Feedback requests from the new updates
- Questions on how to apply the new updates
- Change validations from the new updates
- Findings from denials that impact charging process
- Findings from audits that impact charging process
- Findings from billing reviews that impact charging process
- Findings from CDM review that impact charging process
- Problem-solving charging issues
- Implementation, training, and feedback on new charging process solutions

The appropriate form for each communication type may be determined in the communication plan or may be dictated by the level of urgency of the issue at hand. Regardless, the CDM team should discuss and determine a set of appropriate forms of communication for compliance guidance and issues.

Forms of Communication

It is important to establish in advance what forms of communication are appropriate for compliance guidance and issues. Since a compliance issue may contain sensitive information, the team must set boundaries for communication so that a situation does not spiral out of control. Some standard forms of communication for compliance guidance and issues are:

1. Simple e-mail or interoffice memo
2. Person-to-person informal discussion
3. Ad hoc formal group meeting
4. Quarterly meetings
5. Monthly meetings
6. Weekly meetings

Let's face it, we all get inundated with information from all types of mediums and sources. Critical information gets lost in the piles of information to sort through, read, absorb, and then finally to put into action. The best practice is to funnel all compliance information into one centralized location. That centralized location is then responsible for the reading of all compliance literature and then the triage of the literature by (1) departments impacted, (2) highest risk factor, and (3) urgency of deadline.

That centralized resource is then responsible for sending out the information to the respected departments. To ensure those departments received the literature, have read and understood it, and are ready to put together an action plan, there needs to be regularly scheduled compliance team meetings for review. The frequency of the meetings can vary depending on the time of year, the amount of compliance changes, and the risk factor for implementation of a compliance change as well as the total amount of participants in the charging process. The centralized resource has to be more than one person. If not, then the information can get bottle-necked and cause unnecessary delays due to illness, vacations, or backlog of work. The process has to support the ever-changing dynamic of a hospital informational structure.

Educating Ancillary Departments

The ancillary departments are focused on patient care. Getting the staff from each ancillary department to understand CPT/HCPCS codes, CPT/HCPCS coding rules, federal regulations, state regulations, and payer-specific regulations can be a daunting task. Each hospital has a select number of ancillary staff members that have a good understanding of the overall process for CDM maintenance and compliance. However, some ancillary departments view this as a once-a-year task that they have to perform and then they move back to patient care. The first barrier to overcome is getting the ancillary staff to recognize that compliance review is an ongoing event throughout the year.

At the very least, a staff member from laboratory, radiology, and rehabilitation needs to be on the compliance team. Keep in mind that radiology is broken into multiple specialties and a radiology tech from cat-scan (CT) many not be well-versed in the procedures for nuclear medicine. When specific compliance issues are brought to the team meetings, a nuclear medicine tech may be required to attend the meeting for discussion. The same is true for laboratory and rehabilitation.

Each ancillary can be invited to participate in the compliance meetings. However, the more specialties a hospital offers their patients, the more participants may be included. Each ancillary department needs to have a centralized contact for all compliance, coding, and charging questions. Sometimes these duties are pushed off to the department secretary. While the department administrative assistant may be very efficient in his or her duties, the secretary still does not have the technical knowledge that is needed when reviewing compliance materials, coding questions, or charging processes.

Once you have identified your key contacts for each ancillary department, the next step is to assess their knowledge level of the entire charging process. For those ancillary staff that are new to the process or have limited exposure to the CDM maintenance and compliance, they will need some basic education. It is critical to the ongoing success of a compliance team to have all your team members educated in the basic charging and compliance process. The compliance education that is required for CDM compliance team members is provided in figure 5.9. Education of these important topics can be achieved in many forms.

ICD-9-CM/CPT and HCPCS books	Internet access to CMS, FI, and MAC
American Hospital Association (AHA) Coding Clinics	National Correct Coding Initiative Edits
American Medical Association (AMA) CPT Assistant	Federal Register
HCPCS Newsletter	CDM viewing access
CMS Program Transmittals and Memorandums	Facility charge viewing access
AHA Coding Handbook	LCD and NCD

Source: Clark 2008.

Figure 5.9. Suggested compliance educational materials

Forms of Education

It is important to select the appropriate form of education for your audience. The form of education selected should be based on the type, depth, and amount of information that needs to be understood by the user. And remember that not all individuals learn in the same way. Some may be visual learners, some may be audio learners; therefore, multiple forms may be required for very urgent or very important information. Some common forms of education are:

- Reading training materials
- Reading regulations, policies, and edits
- Attending informal in-services
- Attending internal training sessions
- Reviewing audit or denial reports
- Attending external training sessions
- Attending regular compliance meetings

Helping the ancillary departments understand why the accurate maintenance of the CDM is important will result in a compliant charging environment for the hospital. Compliance is simply the ability of the staff to use the tools, apply the legal rules, and avoid bad decisions due to lack of accurate information. You can have the perfect charge description master, but if your staff does not know how to use it, then it is just a worthless tool. The tool is only as good as the education you provide to those using it. Therefore, a significant amount of time and attention needs to be given to the staff that executes charge entry.

Working with the Compliance Office

All the members of the compliance team need to work closely with the compliance office. It is possible for five separate people to pick up the exact same federal regulation and walk away with a slightly different perspective of how those regulations should be interpreted or implemented. Therefore, before any action plan is implemented, it should be reviewed by the compliance office for mutual agreement of the interpretation of the regulation when there is a discrepancy.

Conversely, the compliance office does not always have a clear picture of exactly how a CDM is used or how the entire charging process is designed. While a regulation may require a specific billing practice for Medicare, it does not always mean that a managed care contract may not require a completely opposite billing practice. All too often we pull federal regulations for Medicare or Medicaid and make the appropriate changes to our CDM, only to learn in our denials departments that several of our managed care payers are denying all the claims impacted by that Medicare change. Compliance has to be viewed at a global perspective and not just at a federal or state level.

The Office of Inspector General (OIG) releases their yearly work plan of those potential areas of high risk for fraud and abuse. The compliance team should be working together to review the OIG work plan and identify those areas of high risk within their individual hospitals.

Monitoring Compliance

Technology has provided multiple resources for tracking, monitoring, and correcting compliance. The challenge is to have staff knowledgeable in the process to interpret the reports from these systems. A denial of a claim may be interpreted by the staff that a new code needs to be added; however, when the HIM coder gets the denied claim it is because the correct diagnosis code used is not considered to be medically necessary by Medicare and therefore the claim is not paid.

Technology is available to monitor compliance at all points of the charging process. The Admitting department can monitor medical necessity along with the Advance Beneficiary Notice technology to reduce denied claims. Ancillary departments can monitor compliance with smart edits in their systems to alert them when they are in violation of NCCI or IOCE edits. HIM departments can monitor compliance with APC grouping logic and encoders. The patient accounting department can monitor compliance through outpatient claim scrubbers and additional smart edits that alert them when they are in violation of billing rules.

Monitoring the compliance can be fairly straightforward. The real challenge is getting the resolution corrected at the beginning of the charging process. Staff on the back end can get complacent about their vital role in correcting errors. Staff will correct the problem on the claim and move forward. Unfortunately, this correction is only good for the one claim and does not address the repeating error or non-compliance. Feedback to the front-end staff, ancillary departments, and CDM maintenance is critical in keeping the hospital charging process fluid and accurate.

The compliance team needs to be aware of these high frequency patterns that are changed so they can address which source it is coming from. The source can be narrowed down to three areas of concentration: Was the error caused by people, by technology, or by the process? When the OIG or any other organization steps foot in your hospital, it is the responsibility of your compliance team to defend your voluntary efforts to be compliant (Hanna 2002). It is important that the team work toward developing a complete and executable compliance plan for the CDM area to ensure compliance is met.

References

3M Health Information System. 2010 (January). *Outpatient Code Editor with Ambulatory Payment Classification Software; Installation and User's Manual.* 3M:Wallingford, CT.

Bowman, S. 2008. *Health Information Management Compliance: Guidelines for Preventing Fraud and Abuse,* 4th ed. Chicago: AHIMA.

Centers for Medicare and Medicaid Services. 2005. Program Transmittals Overview. http://www.cms.hhs.gov/transmittals/01_overview.asp.

Centers for Medicare and Medicaid Services. 2008 (rev. April 25). Medicare Program Integrity Manual: Chapter 13—Local Coverage Determinations. http://www.cms.gov/manuals/downloads/pim83c13.pdf.

Centers for Medicare and Medicaid Services. 2009 (rev. Nov. 13). Medicare Claims Processing Manual. Chapter 23, Section 20.9. http://www.cms.gov/manuals/downloads/clm104c23.pdf.

Centers for Medicare and Medicaid Services. 2010a. Internet-Only Manuals (IOMs). http://www.cms.hhs.gov/Manuals/IOM/list.asp.

Centers for Medicare and Medicaid Services. 2010b (rev. May 28). Medicare National Coverage Determinations Manual: Chapter 1, Part 2 (Sections 90–160.26)—Coverage Determinations. http://www.cms.gov/manuals/downloads/ncd103c1_Part2.pdf.

Centers for Medicare and Medicaid Services. 2010c. National Correct Coding Initiative Policy Manual for Medicare Services. Version 15.3, Chapter 10, page X-5. http://www.cms.hhs.gov/NationalCorrect CodInitEd/.

Centers for Medicare and Medicaid Services. 2010d. Medicare Summary Notices: Overview. http://www.cms.gov/MSN/01_overview.asp#TopOfPage.

Centers for Medicare and Medicaid Services. 2010e. Device, Radiolabeled Product, and Procedure Edits. http://www.cms.gov/HospitalOutpatientPPS/02_device_procedure.asp#TopOfPage.

Clark, A. 2008 (October). Implement IDEAL Outpatient Coding Model: The Essence of Compliance. *Proceedings from AHIMA's 80th National Convention and Exhibit.* Chicago: AHIMA.

Hanna, J. 2002. Constructing a coding compliance plan. *Journal of AHIMA* 73(7):48–56.

Washington Publishing Company. 2010. Code Lists. http://www.wpc-edi.com/codes.

Resources

Centers for Medicare and Medicaid Services. n.d. National Correct Coding Initiative. Modifier -59 Article. https://www.cms.gov/NationalCorrectCodInitEd/; http://www.cms.hhs.gov/NationalCorrect CodInitEd/Downloads/modifier59.pdf.

Cummins, R. and J. Waddell. 2005 (July–August). Coding connections in revenue cycle management. *Journal of AHIMA* 76(7):72–74.

Devault, K. and G. Miller. 2006 (October). Revenue cycle: Relationship with finance and other collaborative relationships. *Proceedings from AHIMA's 78th National Convention and Exhibit.* Chicago: AHIMA.

Drach, M., A. Davis, and C. Sagrati. 2001. Ten steps to successful chargemaster reviews. *Journal of AHIMA* 72(1):42–48.

Hirschl, N. and P. Belton. 2005 (October) Revenue integrity and coding compliance: The sharp experience. *Proceedings from AHIMA's 77th National Convention and Exhibit.* Chicago: AHIMA.

Huber, N., K. Youmans, and T. Wharton. 2004 (October). Improve your organization's financial health: Tools and strategies to manage your revenue cycle. *Proceedings from IFHRO Congress & AHIMA Convention.*

Purcell, L. 2007 (October). Teaching billing compliance to ancillary department managers. *Proceedings from AHIMA's 79th National Convention and Exhibit.* Chicago: AHIMA.

Robinson, C.M. 2007 (October). Coding and patient financial services—Creating a healthy revenue cycle. *Proceedings from AHIMA's 79th National Convention and Exhibit.* Chicago: AHIMA.

Schuler, G. 2003 (October). Auditing and monitoring strategies: Finding lost opportunities. *Proceedings from AHIMA's 75th Anniversary National Convention and Exhibit.* Chicago: AHIMA.

Chapter 6

Corporate Charge Description Masters

Marjery Mazoh, MS

Background

The development and use of corporate charge description masters has grown significantly in the past ten years, in conjunction with expanded attention given to the Chargemaster and the increase of mergers or purchases of individual hospitals into healthcare systems. Just as the individual Chargemaster serves as a comprehensive file of chargeable services and items, the corporate Chargemaster is a comprehensive collection of the same information, on an organization-wide basis. Additionally, the corporate CDM should provide an organization-wide standard for key CDM components, such as CPT/HCPCS coding, assignment of revenue codes, and descriptions. The corporate standard may be used as a suggested or reference source, or may be used to manage or control the individual Chargemaster files, or an organization may use a combination of these approaches. All will depend on the organization's overall Chargemaster strategy and operating model, the underlying billing system or systems, and the technology and tools available. An organization also may adjust the role and structure of the corporate standard as other factors change, such as the implementation of a new billing or revenue-cycle system, the acquisition or opening of a new facility, or with the addition or closing of a clinical service.

Standardization

The general structure and maintenance of a corporate CDM follows the same core Chargemaster concepts described throughout this book. The key components of any corporate standard Chargemaster file will include a charge code (unique identifier), charge description, CPT or HCPCS code where appropriate, and the standard revenue code (Leeds 2001). Depending on the billing system(s) in use, and the overall CDM strategy, the corporate file may also include additional CPT/HCPCS codes and revenue codes if there are payer or financial class-specific billing requirements managed through the Chargemaster. The corporate file may also include a standard price, as well as payer identifiers, modifiers, and other data elements used in Chargemasters. The corporate CDM should contain at least one instance of **all** codes and items contained in the individual CDMs of the health system that are to be included in whatever corporate model the organization adopts. The organization may decide to have separate departments, to match existing department or general ledger codes in the local Chargemasters, or to reflect a clinical service line (for example, Surgery, Pharmacy, and Women's Health) for purposes of matching services across hospitals. Or the organization may elect to have only one occurrence of each item, code, or service to be shared across all departments or service lines.

Some key benefits of developing and using a corporate standard include improved efficiency, increased consistency, and transparency (Barton 2007). A fully integrated corporate Chargemaster, particularly one used with a robust software product, can facilitate a more streamlined updating and management of all of the system's Chargemasters. This is especially true during the process of completing the annual code updates, where the organization adds new codes and updates deleted and replaced codes in the master file; and then uses the software to migrate the changes to all of the local hospital files, rather than having to build or update in each file separately.

This centralized management also improves the consistency of the data in each separate Chargemaster, because it is maintained once in a central file, rather than relying on repeated keystrokes. With each additional manual touch of a data field, the risk increases that there will be typographical errors, variations in spacing, and other differences that can impact having a consistent, correct individual Chargemaster.

Finally, with an efficient process and clean, consistent data, the level of information transparency increases significantly, improving the ability for staff to identify information across facilities and better communicating it to patients on bills and other documents. Charge descriptions may now look the same across hospitals, so that clinical staff that float to different facilities see the same description consistently. Patients who receive services at different facilities may see more consistent information on billing communications. Staff looking at the Chargemaster or related files throughout the organization may more easily identify similar services more quickly, to support whatever information or analytical needs they have.

Many organizations have found that with the implementation of their corporate standard and a more centralized operation for maintaining the Chargemaster, particularly in conjunction with supporting technology, they can now focus more time on other revenue cycle functions. Many Chargemaster groups have moved from focusing almost exclusively on updating Chargemasters to working more with clinical departments to identify charge capture opportunities, revenue assurance projects, and further integration or support to other areas.

Some of the risks or challenges of using a corporate Chargemaster standard include resistance to change, differing government and commercial payer requirements, and the amount of work and time required to begin the process and fully implement. Making the move from separate hospital Chargemasters and processes to an integrated or centralized Chargemaster, in whatever form and to whatever extent the organization determines they need, will likely be a significant change from the current state for all impacted. Even when everyone understands the need for and agrees with the overall strategy of moving in this direction, it still presents challenges. Similarly, Chargemaster staff may be concerned about potential job loss with a change in the operating model. As described above, if the organization anticipates that there will be additional opportunities or different work in a broader revenue cycle or revenue integrity function, this might be part of the early project communication as well. It is important whenever possible to describe the future state model as early as possible, so that team members can focus on the project rather than their future role. It is equally important to integrate communication and engagement and change management in this work as it is to develop standard descriptions and coding methods.

The regulatory and payer environment adds an additional risk or challenge to the efficiencies gained from a corporate Chargemaster, especially for organizations with hospitals in multiple states or regions. Individual hospitals often are challenged by managing a single Chargemaster in an area where government and commercial payers have differing requirements for the use of HCPCS Level II versus CPT codes, or for different revenue codes. These requirements may be managed through the Chargemaster, through other functionality in the billing system, through claim edits, or some combination of all of these. When integrating the Chargemaster structure and function across multiple hospitals in the same region, health systems often find variability in how the individual hospitals have managed these differences. Taking this variability across multiple regions increases the probability of exceptions, and may require additional planning and maintenance at the corporate level. At a minimum, it is critical to assess these factors when developing the plan and structure for the corporate standard, before beginning to conform individual hospital Chargemasters to a single set of rules if those rules will not work or will create downstream rework, denials, or other new breakpoints in existing revenue cycle processes.

Developing and implementing a corporate standard Chargemaster often takes a minimum of one year, with many organizations reporting that it has taken two years or more to complete the work involved. The initial phases require a combination of intense attention to detail with a broad strategic approach, as well as project management and data management skills to manage all of the pieces effectively. Implementation and ongoing maintenance require additional planning and oversight, in order to ensure that the standard is applied consistently and updated appropriately going forward. Many organizations engage consultants or other outside assistance for some or all of this work, as the internal team often does not have sufficient, protected time or the full skill set to manage the entire project. Wherever possible, it is advised to involve the existing Chargemaster team and other key stakeholders (clinical directors, billing team members, others as appropriate) in as much of the project as possible. They bring subject matter expertise on the current state of Chargemaster and related processes, on individual clinical areas, and they are key to generating buy in of whatever new model is developed. They also will play a critical role in the implementation and ongoing maintenance of the corporate standard, so it is helpful to include them as early as possible in the process, even when working with outside resources.

Before building a corporate CDM, the organization should assess and outline the desired strategy and plan for using the corporate CDM. If it is intended, for example, to be a reference document for all hospitals to use to see what services they might include, and how to describe and code them, then the approach might be to combine information from all existing files, reduce duplicate items, and store the information in a central location for all to reference.

In contrast, if the organization intends to use the corporate Chargemaster to develop, implement, and manage a standard set of descriptions, codes, and other information, it is important to have a more comprehensive approach. First, it will be important to determine which fields need to be standardized. It may be possible to migrate all CDMs to one of the existing files, particularly if an existing Chargemaster is already comprehensive and complete. Or, the organization may choose to develop a "Best Practices CDM" to use to update all sites. Much will depend on the current status of each of the existing CDMs, and whether there is one that is already considered to be complete and comprehensive enough to use for all hospitals. Similarly, if an organization has multiple billing platforms, the corporate file may only include the fields that are shared by all systems, with the additional or unique fields maintained separately. The corporate file may still contain all fields from all billing systems, but it may become rather unwieldy and difficult to maintain effectively.

Charge Description

Frequently, when an organization begins comparing existing CDMs in preparation for developing the corporate standard, it will find that the same service or charge code has very different descriptions across the different hospitals. Although CDM charge descriptions do not have any regulatory requirements and do not directly impact payment, this piece of a standardization project often takes a great deal of time and energy early in the project (Bielby, et al. 2010). While it may seem frustrating and wasteful, it is an important part of the work and has many non-payment-related benefits. In addition, finding a standard way to clearly and concisely describe services may be more difficult than expected. If current descriptions appear on patient bills, or are used on charge tickets or order screens, they may be confusing or unclear, or may be what clinical staff have become accustomed to using when selecting what they are ordering or have provided. Before changing and implementing new descriptions, it is important to gain an understanding of how the current descriptions were developed, how and where they are being used, what the potential impact of changing them will be, and whether they need to change in all places or only in some places. As an example, some hospitals find that they can maintain existing descriptions on order entry or service screens, while updating within the Chargemaster and billing system. Table 6.1 provides an example of this strategy. This minimizes disruption to clinical staff, while improving what patients see on their statements. If this is not possible or is not the organization's strategy, then it is helpful to involve key clinical staffs who use the information to develop the parameters for the new information.

It is useful to spend some time early in the project determining standard abbreviations to use for frequently used words, such as "blood," "additional," "fracture," and the like. The same code used in different departments should have the same description, and the same word used in different descriptions should be abbreviated the same way consistently. Again, it is a tremendous amount of detail that does not impact reimbursement, but it does impact the ability to understand and communicate across locations.

Revenue Code Assignment

Another key consideration at the beginning of the standardization process is how many standard revenue codes to assign, and how to determine them. The question of how many stems from the existing Chargemasters, billing systems, and payer requirements. The corporate revenue code should be based on how the organization determines the default revenue code that is stored, whether it is for Medicare, for a specific commercial payer, from an internal best practices determination, and such. Some billing systems hold only one revenue code, so the corporate standard would likely hold only one as well, unless there are different requirements for specific payers that the organization wants to store as reference material in the corporate file. If the billing systems already store multiple revenue codes, then the organization can determine if they want to incorporate and maintain these in the corporate file or not.

Table 6.1. Clinical Charge Descriptions versus Standard CDM Charge Descriptions

Depart-ment Number	Charge Code	Clinical Charge Description	Revenue Code	HCPCS Code	Price	Standard CDM Charge Descrip-tion
500	5204116	CL TX EL-BOW DISLO W/O ANES	450	24600	$1,365.00	Closed fracture care, elbow
500	5004119	CL TX RAD HD/NECK FX W/O MAN	450	24650	$992.00	Closed fracture care, radius
500	5004120	CL TX RAD HD/NECK FX W/MAN	450	24655	$1,932.00	Closed fracture care, radius
500	5004121	CL TX ULNAR FX PROX W/O MAN	450	24670	$1,274.00	Closed fracture care, ulna
500	5204122	CL TX ULNAR FX PROX W/MAN	450	24675	$2,365.00	Closed fracture care, ulna
500	5204127	CL TX RAD SH FX W/O MAN	450	25500	$1,071.00	Closed fracture care, radius
500	5204128	CL TX RAD SH FX W/MAN	450	25505	$2,509.00	Closed fracture care, radius
500	5204129	CL TX RAD SH FX W/DIS JNT	450	25520	$3,362.00	Closed fracture care, radius
500	5204130	CL TX ULNAR SH FX W/O MAN	450	25530	$992.00	Closed fracture care, ulna
500	5004131	CL TX ULNAR SH FX W/MAN	450	25535	$2,499.00	Closed fracture care, ulna
500	5004132	CL TX RAD ULNAR FX W/O MAN	450	25560	$1,284.00	Closed fracture care, radius-ulna
500	5004133	CL TX RAD ULNAR FX W/MAN	450	25565	$2,902.00	Closed fracture care, radius-ulna

Depart- ment Number	Charge Code	Clinical Charge Description	Revenue Code	HCPCS Code	Price	Standard CDM Charge Descrip- tion
500	5204134	CL TX DIS RAD FX W/O MAN	450	25600	$1,132.00	Closed fracture care, radius
500	5204135	CL TX DIS RAD FX W/ WO FX ULN	450	25605	$2,075.00	Closed fracture care, radius
500	5004136	CL TX CAR-PAL SCAP FX W/O MAN	450	25622	$1,123.00	Closed fracture care, carpal
500	5204137	CL TX CAR-PAL SCAP FX W/MAN	450	25624	$1,961.00	Closed fracture care, carpal
500	5204138	CL TX CAR-PAL FX W/O MAN EACH	450	25630	$1,180.00	Closed fracture care, carpal
500	5004139	CL TX CAR-PAL FX W/ MAN EACH	450	25635	$1,874.00	Closed fracture care, carpal
500	5004140	CL TX ULNAR STYLOID FX	450	25650	$1,289.00	Closed fracture care, ulna
500	5004141	CL TX RAD/ INTERCAR DIS W/MAN	450	25660	$1,926.00	Closed fracture care, radius
500	5004142	CL TX DIST RAD DIS W/ MAN	450	25675	$2,016.00	Closed fracture care, radius
500	5204150	CL TX CAR-POMET DIS THB W/MAN	450	26641	$1,491.00	Closed fracture care, carpo-metacarpal
500	5204151	CL TX CAR-POMET FX THB W/MAN	450	26645	$1,936.00	Closed fracture care, carpo-metacarpal

Continued

Table 6.1.　Clinical Charge Descriptions versus Standard CDM Charge Descriptions
(Continued)

Depart-ment Number	Charge Code	Clinical Charge Description	Revenue Code	HCPCS Code	Price	Standard CDM Charge Descrip-tion
500	5004152	CL TX CAR-POMET DIS SNG W/MAN	450	26670	$1,375.00	Closed fracture care, carpo-metacarpal
500	5204153	CL TX META-CAR DIS SNG W/MAN	450	26700	$1,168.00	Closed fracture care, meta-carpal
500	5204155	CL TX PHAL SH FX W/O MAN EACH	450	26720	$663.00	Closed fracture care, pha-lange
500	5204156	CL TX PHAL SH FX W/ MAN/TR EACH	450	26725	$928.00	Closed fracture care, pha-lange
500	5004159	CL TX DIS PHAL FX W/O MAN EA	450	26750	$739.00	Closed fracture care, pha-lange
500	5204160	CL TX DIS PHAL FX W/ MAN EACH	450	26755	$1,338.00	Closed fracture care, pha-lange
500	5204161	CL TX INTER-PHAL JNT DISL W/MAN	450	26770	$823.00	Closed fracture care, pha-langeal joint

CPT/HCPCS Codes

Similar to the revenue code assignment decisions previously described, if the billing systems currently store more than one CPT/HCPCS (that is, for Medicare versus commercial payers), then the corporate file can be designed similarly.

Pricing

If the health system has standardized prices (charges) for all lines in their Charge-masters, then price should be a mandatory field in the corporate Chargemaster so that they can use it to populate the price in the individual files. If the health system has standardized prices for some lines, such as supplies or operating room time, then they may wish to have this as a field in the corporate Chargemaster that does not automatically populate the individual files. If there are no standardized prices, then the health system can decide whether they want to store a suggested or reference price, or skip this field entirely.

Code Changes

Once the fields are determined and the basic rules decided, the next set of considerations include plans for change management, such as the addition, replacement, or deletion of CPT and HCPCS Level II codes, the addition or discontinuation of services, hard coding versus soft coding, and modifiers. Again, some of these decisions may be straightforward based on existing CDM set up and practices, but for a health system where there is variation among their hospitals, these should be reviewed and decided early. Throughout the development, implementation, and ongoing maintenance of the corporate standard, there will also be situations that require additional review. If the corporate CDM is used to control the content of the local CDMs, then timely and accurate updates after code changes become even more crucial, as the one file now drives multiple files. Failure to update the corporate CDM could result in multiple locations failing to send correct bills, which increases the negative impact of Chargemaster-driven denials. Therefore, it is recommended that the organization have a clear strategy and plan for managing code updates; this may mirror existing practice for the individual hospitals or may need to be developed differently.

Adding and Deleting Codes

When a new service is added or an old service is discontinued, it is crucial to have a plan and process for the timely update of the corporate Chargemaster. Whether this includes just one line or an entire department, the quality of the data again can impact multiple hospitals. For the addition of new codes, there should be a process and policy that describe who may request an addition and how, what validation occurs, and then how it will be built in the corporate file. This would include the naming convention, how and if a service code is assigned, the assignment of the CPT/HCPCS code(s) and revenue code(s), and the pricing, if applicable. If a service is discontinued, following existing policy on the timing of CDM inactivation, the corporate file should be adjusted appropriately.

Hard versus Soft Coding

As an organization embarks on developing a corporate Chargemaster, this is frequently an area of additional review. Depending on charge capture and coding practices in existing departments across the organization, it may or may not be an issue. It does frequently come up in areas such as GI/endoscopy, cardiac catheterization, and interventional radiology. If the GI lab performs an upper GI endoscopy with biopsy, the nurse or physician may select a specific CDM to match the exact procedure they did, which will then add the specific CPT code to the bill (hard coding), or during or after the procedure a coder reviews the procedure notes and selects the CPT code that matches the procedure, and appends it to a more general procedure CDM (soft coding). Neither approach is better than the other—it depends on the knowledge of the staff selecting the codes, the level of specificity or generality of the Chargemaster, and the checks in place to ensure that the coding is accurate.

Where this gets difficult in the corporate Chargemaster context, however, is where the hospitals in one system approach this type of situation differently. If some use soft coding in an area where others use hard coding, the corporate standard Chargemaster needs to be built to accommodate two different approaches, or the coding and charging approach needs to change at some locations to be standard. See table 6.2 for an illustration of varying approaches.

Impacts of Changes in Charge Practice and Structure

The corporate CDM project team may or may not have accountability for or involvement in revenue budgets, cost accounting, decision support, and other areas that are impacted by changes in charge structure, but it is important to consider these areas and involve stakeholders in this process. When significant changes are made to the Chargemaster, revenue may increase or decrease beyond expected parameters. The organization may want to adjust prices to offset these shifts.

Changes to the Chargemaster may also impact reporting parameters, resulting in under- or overcounting utilization data. Again, it may be helpful to involve members

Table 6.2.   Interventional Radiology Coding Strategy

	Hospital A		Hospital B		Hospital C	
	Radiology	**Surgery**	**Radiology**	**Surgery**	**Radiology**	**Surgery**
Hard coded			X		X	X
Soft coded	X	X		X		

of the decision support team to allow them to anticipate potential impact and adjust models or monitor for potential changes. Clinical and charge entry staff also need to be educated about the changes being made to the charge structure, and clinical information systems or other charge vehicles may need to be updated to support the new structure.

Case Study I – Midwest Medical Center

Midwest Medical Center (Midwest) is a multi-hospital system formed ten years ago from the merger of a large academic medical center, a smaller four-hospital system, and four additional community hospitals. Across Midwest, there are three different billing systems with very different Chargemaster structures. Although early preparations are under way for the implementation of a shared billing platform, it is not expected to be complete for three to five years. Over the past ten years, each hospital has developed a separate Chargemaster management process. Two years ago, the system purchased a Chargemaster software tool, which was the first shared tool ever in this system. With the implementation of this shared tool, the hospitals are able to view each other's Chargemasters for the first time. As the organization moves toward fuller integration and increased transparency for patients, providers, and employees, one piece of that strategy is to develop a corporate Chargemaster to standardize their codes and descriptions. Additionally, the shared technology will allow the organization to actively manage and maintain all of the Chargemasters through a single corporate team instead of separate individuals working in isolation. The corporate Chargemaster file is also expected to serve as the foundation for the Chargemaster in the future integration to a single billing system.

At the beginning of the corporate standardization process, there were no shared rules for the Chargemasters. Descriptions were completely different, as were many revenue code assignments. Each billing system had different functionality around the number of CPT/HCPCS codes, revenue codes, and the length of descriptions to be held, and the combined total of all of the Chargemasters included over 100,000 active lines. Because of the size and complexity of the work required, Midwest engaged an outside consultant to support the data analysis and overall project management.

The project team was a combined group of consultants and the Chargemaster subject matter experts from Midwest's hospitals. The group worked closely together to develop guiding principles and working tools for the project. Some of this time included consensus development on naming conventions for descriptions and standard abbreviations. One of the very first guiding principles was to build a completely new "best practices" corporate Chargemaster. This new corporate Chargemaster would draw from all of the existing Chargemasters, comparing between the hospitals and comparing to similar organizations.

Because the length of descriptions used in each billing system can vary, the team decided to limit the corporate description to the *shortest* length allowed by any system, and consistently applied this constraint to all work going forward. Similarly, the team tried to develop this information in a format that would make sense to clinical personnel, as many of the order entry systems would also contain these descriptions. The team members worked with clinical representatives throughout the project to review the proposed descriptions to make sure they made sense to clinical staff as well. This was time consuming but assisted in laying the groundwork for the adoption of the descriptions when implemented.

The team then worked to develop project departments based on general clinical services to break the 100,000 lines and multiple departments into more workable pieces. Some of these included Emergency Services, Lab, Imaging, and Cardiology. Each hospital's billing departments were assigned to a single project department. Where there was overlap of services, such as cardiac services provided in interventional radiology, the team reviewed the IR services first during the cardiac review, and again during the imaging review to assure full review.

Over a period of about a year, the team worked its way through each project department. The consultants provided an initial draft of proposed standards, including charge descriptions, CPT/HCPCS codes, and revenue codes, which was then reviewed by each team member with representatives from the clinical departments. This review also included flagging items without volume for two years, to consider inactivation, and flagging items that appeared to be duplicates, to consider combining with other existing lines. Changes were collected and integrated to an interim draft, which went for an additional review. The consultants then compared the project department and each hospital to each other and to similar organizations to identify potential charge items that may need to be added.

As each project department was finalized, Midwest's Chargemaster team received a final Chargemaster file that was used as the basis for building the corporate Chargemaster within the software tool. This corporate file was described as a "virtual Chargemaster," because it existed only within the software tool and in an off-system database, maintained by the department director. It did not reside in any billing or other standard information system. This was chosen as the operating model for Midwest because of the significant differences in the billing systems described previously.

Each line in the corporate department was then linked to the appropriate lines in the individual hospital Chargemasters, and the software functionality was able to propagate the changes to each hospital. As the changes were integrated, the individual Chargemasters began to more closely resemble each other, allowing for more meaningful analysis and reporting across the organization. As the implementation came to an end, Midwest's team began moving into maintaining the core Chargemaster fields for all of the hospitals via the technology and linking from the corporate file. Because of the differences in the billing systems, they continue to do additional maintenance in each separate Chargemaster as well, but it drives from the overall corporate standard.

Table 6.3 illustrates the impact that CDM standardization has on each facility as discussed in this case study. The table shows how the use of a corporate or "virtual Chargemaster" resulted in modifications to the CDMs at each facility. This table is a sample view; it includes a look at emergency department visit levels for three facilities.

Table 6.3. Sample CDMs Pre versus Post Corporate Standardization

Hospital A before Corporate CDM Standardization

Department Number	Charge Code	Charge Description	Revenue Code	HCPCS Code
400	7204008	EMERGENCY LEVEL I	450	99281
400	7204009	EMERGENCY LEVEL II	450	99282
400	7204010	EMERGENCY LEVEL III	450	99283
400	7204011	EMERGENCY LEVEL IV	450	99284
400	7204012	EMERGENCY LEVEL V	450	99285
400	7204013	EMERGENCY CRITICAL CARE I	450	99291
400	7204014	EMERGENCY CRITICAL CARE II	450	99292

Hospital B before Corporate CDM Standardization

Department Number	Charge Code	Charge Description	Revenue Code	HCPCS Code
255	8104009	TYPE A ED 1	450	99281
255	8104502	TYPE B ED 1	450	99281
255	8104010	TYPE A ED 2	450	99282
255	8104503	TYPE B ED 2	450	99282
255	8104011	TYPE A ED 3	450	99283
255	8104504	TYPE B ED 3	450	99283
255	8104012	TYPE A ED 4	450	99284
255	8104505	TYPE B ED 4	450	99284
255	8104013	TYPE A ED 5	450	99285
255	8104506	TYPE B ED 5	450	99285
255	8104014	CRITICAL CARE 30-74 MIN	450	99291
255	8104015	CRITICAL CARE ADD'L 30 MIN	450	99292

Continued

Table 6.3.   Sample CDMs Pre versus Post Corporate Standardization *(Continued)*

Hospital C before Corporate CDM Standardization				
Department Number	**Charge Code**	**Charge Description**	**Revenue Code**	**HCPCS Code**
357	3570001	ED LEVEL 1	450	99281
357	3570002	ED LEVEL 2	450	99282
357	3570003	ED LEVEL 3	450	99283
357	3570004	ED LEVEL 4	450	99284
357	3570005	ED LEVEL 5	450	99285
Corporate CDM (Virtual Chargemaster)				
Department Number	**Charge Code**	**Charge Description**	**Revenue Code**	**HCPCS Code**
720	7204001	EMERGENCY LEVEL 1	450	99281
720	7204002	TYPE B EMERGENCY LEVEL 1	450	99281
720	7204003	EMERGENCY LEVEL 2	450	99282
720	7204004	TYPE B EMERGENCY LEVEL 2	450	99282
720	7204005	EMERGENCY LEVEL 3	450	99283
720	7204006	TYPE B EMERGENCY LEVEL 3	450	99283
720	7204007	EMERGENCY LEVEL 4	450	99284
720	7204008	TYPE B EMERGENCY LEVEL 4	450	99284
720	7204009	EMERGENCY LEVEL 5	450	99285
720	7204010	TYPE B EMERGENCY LEVEL 5	450	99285
720	7204012	CRITICAL CARE 30-74 MIN	450	99291
720	7204013	CRITICAL CARE ADD'L 30 MIN	450	99292
Hospital A after Corporate CDM Standardization				
Department Number	**Charge Code**	**Charge Description**	**Revenue Code**	**HCPCS Code**
720	7204001	EMERGENCY LEVEL 1	450	99281
720	7204003	EMERGENCY LEVEL 2	450	99282
720	7204005	EMERGENCY LEVEL 3	450	99283
720	7204007	EMERGENCY LEVEL 4	450	99284
720	7204009	EMERGENCY LEVEL 5	450	99285
720	7204012	CRITICAL CARE 30-74 MIN	450	99291
720	7204013	CRITICAL CARE ADD'L 30 MIN	450	99292

Hospital B after Corporate CDM Standardization				
Department Number	**Charge Code**	**Charge Description**	**Revenue Code**	**HCPCS Code**
720	7204001	EMERGENCY LEVEL 1	450	99281
720	7204002	TYPE B EMERGENCY LEVEL 1	450	99281
720	7204003	EMERGENCY LEVEL 2	450	99282
720	7204004	TYPE B EMERGENCY LEVEL 2	450	99282
720	7204005	EMERGENCY LEVEL 3	450	99283
720	7204006	TYPE B EMERGENCY LEVEL 3	450	99283
720	7204007	EMERGENCY LEVEL 4	450	99284
720	7204008	TYPE B EMERGENCY LEVEL 4	450	99284
720	7204009	EMERGENCY LEVEL 5	450	99285
720	7204010	TYPE B EMERGENCY LEVEL 5	450	99285
720	7204012	CRITICAL CARE 30-74 MIN	450	99291
720	7204013	CRITICAL CARE ADD'L 30 MIN	450	99292
Hospital C after Corporate CDM Standardization				
Department Number	**Charge Code**	**Charge Description**	**Revenue Code**	**HCPCS Code**
720	7204001	EMERGENCY LEVEL 1	450	99281
720	7204003	EMERGENCY LEVEL 2	450	99282
720	7204005	EMERGENCY LEVEL 3	450	99283
720	7204007	EMERGENCY LEVEL 4	450	99284
720	7204009	EMERGENCY LEVEL 5	450	99285

Case Study II — Mercy Health System

Mercy Health System (Mercy) is a multi-hospital system formed ten years ago from the merger of two hospitals. During the past five years, Mercy has grown to a six-hospital system through the acquisition of four individual hospitals in neighboring states. As each hospital joined Mercy, they moved onto the billing system in use at the other Mercy hospitals. Mercy is now looking to streamline the Chargemaster maintenance process.

Mercy chartered an internal project team that included their Chargemaster leads, revenue cycle managers, health information management representatives, and information systems personnel. They began their work by developing a combined database of all of the active lines in their individual Chargemasters. When each hospital came up on

Mercy's billing system, they also adopted the lines from the Chargemaster that applied to their hospital, so there was some overlap in charge descriptions, CPT/HCPCS codes, and revenue codes. However, after initial implementation, each hospital was managing their Chargemaster independently, so the charge descriptions on items added after that time did not match.

Mercy's team agreed to develop a standard description methodology that all would use all existing and new Chargemaster lines. They based their methodology on recommendations from the Patient Friendly Billing project, in preparation for a new patient-statement system that was expected to go live during the Chargemaster standardization. They wanted patients to be better able to understand the information on their bills and related communications.

The team also felt that because of the different states that they worked in, having one single set of CPT/HCPCS codes and revenue codes for all of the hospitals would not be workable. They wanted the corporate standard to be a reference guide for each hospital to use, but not a requirement, except for charge descriptions. To assist in future Chargemaster development and updating, however, they agreed to develop the standard data file with fields for the preferred or required values for CPT/HCPCS codes and revenue codes for each of the states. This would add many more fields to the corporate standard that would require maintenance, but all felt it would be helpful for guiding future work. Additionally, Mercy's managed care and government relations teams were interested in being able to see the information, to assist in understanding and describing the existing variations in billing requirements across their service area. This was expected to be of great assistance in negotiating with contracted payers who insured patients in multiple states served by Mercy, with the hope of standardizing the contract terms, and thereby decreasing the need for multiple Chargemaster maintenance approaches, claim edits, and such.

The Mercy team also wanted to be able to use the corporate standard as a shared reference for an internal best practices or benchmark. By seeing what services the same clinical area at other hospitals had in their chargemaster, they hoped to encourage their departments to look more closely at their services to determine if there were additional and appropriate charging opportunities. They also hoped this would help in educating clinical staff about services that were not being charged because of compliance or other reasons, to support them in denying these requests.

The pricing team at Mercy also looked forward to having a shared reference, so that they would be able to assign a price once and have it readily available to the Chargemaster teams when adding an existing charge line to a service at a different hospital.

As the team began working on developing their corporate standard, they also used their Chargemaster software tool to build the corporate file for reference. They used a similar linking approach as the team at Midwest but flagged the links as recommendations instead of requirements. As they continued their progress, each of the Chargemaster analysts from the separate hospitals found that their daily tasks related to adding, updating, and maintaining existing Chargemaster lines was getting easier and taking less time. They became concerned that they did not have enough work and would face job reduction or elimination. Then they reminded each other about the other projects related to charge capture and revenue assurance that had been delayed or put aside because of the large amount of manual work they were doing. They dusted off some projects and started expanding their scope of work. Through this renewed effort, and with the added view of the best practices Chargemaster, each of the hospitals identified a number of opportunities to improve their revenue capture.

As the teams at Midwest and at Mercy began working on developing their corporate Chargemaster and the supporting operating model, they needed to consider everything from guiding principles to detailed operational plans. The guiding principles provided the overall framework and context for the corporate Chargemaster, while the detailed operational plans addressed how to make it happen. Some of the high-level considerations included determining whether the corporate standard will be a suggestion or a requirement; whether all fields within the standard will be required or if any will be optional or suggestions; or whether the corporate standard will be used as a central control or management tool for all of the hospitals, or if it will be more of a reference tool only. Similarly, the level of detail within the corporate file was evaluated early to determine whether it will contain only those key fields that are standardized and linked, or whether it will contain all fields present in any one of the local Chargemasters, or some middle ground of key fields and unique or separate fields. These decisions were guided by each organization's overall operating model.

Summary

As health systems continue to grow and integrate, the focus on corporate Chargemasters will also continue to expand. Whether a system is looking to standardize or develop internal best practices, the corporate Chargemaster is a powerful part of the organization's revenue cycle toolkit.

References

Barton, S. and M. Bieker. 2007 (September). Super standardization: One health system, one charge-master. *Healthcare Financial Management* 61(9):74–80.

Bielby, Judy A., et al. Care and maintenance of charge masters. *Journal of AHIMA* (Updated March 2010). http://library.ahima.org/xpedio/groups/public/document/ahima/bok1_047258. hcsp?dDocName=bok1_04728.

Leeds, E. 2001 (October). When good chargemasters go bad. *Proceedings from AHIMA's 73rd National Convention*. Chicago: AHIMA.

Chapter 7

Charge Description Master Audits

John Richey, MBA, RHIA

Purpose

Earlier chapters in this text review and discuss important aspects of Charge Description Master (CDM) management such as CDM structure, maintenance, workflow, and compliance. The Centers for Medicare and Medicaid Services (CMS) requires that all healthcare entities develop and implement a compliance program. One of the key components of a compliance program is periodic CDM auditing.

Regardless of what is being audited, reviewing for accuracy is the most important part, but value-added auditing is more than just a review. Value-added auditing is a systematic, disciplined approach to evaluate and improve the effectiveness of risk management, control, and governance processes (IIA 2010). Value-added auditing has a focus and a purpose, the results of which yield information that is actionable; facilitate education and communication among stakeholders; and enhance an organization's overall compliance, giving it a better handle on its financial operations. Therefore, for many practitioners, this phrase describes audit work that helps management improve the business, rather than assignments that simply verify compliance with policies and procedures. (Roth 1)

This chapter focuses on value-added CDM auditing as a critical component of the healthcare organization's compliance program. CDM auditing will be presented from two standpoints, internal audits and external audits, both of which are critical to compliance.

Internal Audits

Internal audits are performed by person(s) employed by the organization. Larger organizations typically have a department known as the compliance department or auditing department, which staffs one or more auditors. External audits are performed by persons not employed by the organization, but typically through contractual arrangements. External audits will be discussed later in the chapter.

Considerations

Successful audits do not just happen. Careful consideration should be given to the following factors to make certain that the audit will yield the best results for the organization:

- Goal: What is the overall goal of the CDM audit? The main goal of any CDM audit is to validate accuracy to support compliance and the revenue cycle. It is possible that there could be additional goals, such as to yield information to support staff education and training.
- Scope: Is the audit to be broad in scope, looking at the entire CDM and every field within it? Or is the audit to be targeted or limited, for example to just certain fields within the CDM, or to the CDM items in one specific department, or to high-volume, high-risk procedures and services? The broader the scope, the more resources required to complete the audit.
- Frequency: How often will audits occur? The entire CDM should be reviewed annually. Targeted CDM audits should occur more frequently, such as the CDM of a newly opened department or service, which could contain dozens or even hundreds of new charge items.
- Budget and resources: What funds are available to support the audit? Has the department or organization budgeted sufficiently to assure successful completion of the auditing effort? As mentioned earlier, the broader the scope of the audit, the more resources required to complete the audit.
- Staff: How many staff will be required to support ongoing auditing? What are the required education, credentials, and skills sets for the staff?
- Space: Is adequate work space available for staff to perform their duties? Do any modifications need to be made to accommodate their needs? Is there adequate lighting, heating, ventilation, air conditioning? Is there adequate table or desk space?
- Equipment: Is the available equipment sufficient to support staff needs? Are computers available and are the speed, hardware, and software robust enough to meet staff needs?
- Supplies: Are software programs available to staff to support the auditing effort? Are reference materials available?

Once these questions are answered, then the audit can be designed and conducted.

Designing an Audit

Audit design is driven by the goal, scope, and frequency considerations. The main goal of any CDM audit is to validate accuracy and consistency to support claim submission, compliance, and the revenue cycle. The CDM audit with the broadest scope is the audit of the entire CDM, in which every field is reviewed and validated. For large organizations this can be a daunting challenge, requiring many resources, which is why this review is usually performed no more than annually. Most audits will be narrower in scope. For example, if the CPT code for a given service is changed, then a review of only the charge description and CPT code fields is warranted. There are several factors that drive audit frequency. One is periodic CPT code additions, changes, or deletions by the American Medical Association (AMA). As new CPT codes are created, old ones deleted, and others modified, CPT codes within the CDM must also be changed to assure compliance. Additionally, HCPCS Level II codes are updated by CMS yearly and should also be considered for addition, modification, or deletion from the CDM. The CPT/HCPCS code fields within the CDM must be audited every time official CPT/HCPCS code changes are published. Another factor which drives audit frequency is public and private payer guidelines. Payers will periodically issue National Coverage Determinations (NCDs) or Local Coverage Determinations (LCDs), in which they communicate changes to payment rules for various healthcare procedures and services. As each new NCD or LCD is published, the CDM items for such services must be audited to assure compliance with the most current rules. Other factors that drive audit frequency include quarterly and yearly changes to the prospective payment system, periodic changes to the Office of the Inspector General (OIG) Work Plan, and the National Correct Coding Initiative (NCCI). Therefore, it is not uncommon for multiple audits to be occurring simultaneously. Ultimately, once the goal, scope, and frequency of an audit have been determined, the audit can be designed by allocating the necessary staff, space, equipment, and supplies resources to actually conduct the audit.

Steps to Conducting an Audit

There are a series of steps that should be followed in sequence to assure that an audit actually yields favorable results. Figure 7.1 provides a flow chart for internal audits. The following sections address each of the steps that should be taken for a CDM audit.

Stakeholder Agreement

First, the CDM stakeholders should meet to reach alignment (agreement) on the goal(s), scope, and frequency of the planned audit and to coordinate the audit effort. The stakeholders are persons who have a vested interest in the outcome of the audit. They are typically persons with management responsibilities over functional areas

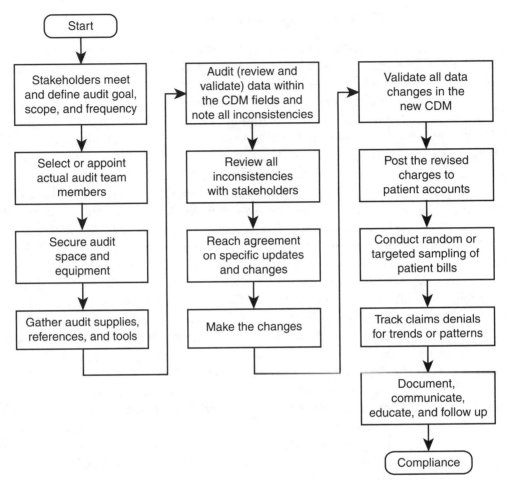

Figure 7.1. Sequential steps in conducting a CDM audit

involved, and can be regarded as subject matter experts in their respective areas of responsibility. At a minimum, the following stakeholders should participate:

- Compliance officer or representative: The organization's compliance officer should spearhead the CDM audit effort, with the overarching goal of assuring accuracy and consistency to support compliance and the revenue cycle. He or she participates as needed to remove barriers, foster communication, and provide leadership and direction.
- Finance department representative: This person typically coordinates the audit effort, schedules stakeholder meetings, conducts the actual audit, reports audit findings, makes the corrections in the CDM, and handles post-audit communications and follow-ups.

- Health Information Management (HIM) representative: This individual is a CPT/HCPCS coding subject matter expert who helps determine which CPT/HCPCS codes will be hard-coded into the CDM and which will be soft-coded or assigned by coders in the HIM department. The HIM representative also reaches alignment with the clinicians on the best CPT/HCPCS code to be assigned to a given procedure or services.
- Clinicians and ancillary department heads: These people are clinical procedure and service subject matter experts. They work with the HIM representative to confirm that the proposed CPT/HCPCS code for a given service matches the description of the actual services rendered. Staff in the clinical departments also enter orders and post charges to patient accounts during or shortly after the patient visit. Accuracy at the charge posting level is a critical point in the revenue cycle.
- Business Office and Business Services representative: An expert on reimbursement and payer guidelines, this individual has access to the latest payer guidelines, has detailed information on past and recent claims denials, and also has detailed information on allowable data within certain fields in the CDM.
- Contracts department representative: This person is a managed care contracts subject matter expert. He or she has access to all relevant managed care contracts, which detail certain contract-specific pricing and CPT/HCPCS coding requirements.
- IT representatives (larger environments): Experts in hardware, software, and network support, they deploy computers in the office environment, provide hardware and software set-up and application support, and may assist in report-writing and data mining. IT staff who directly support computer applications that link to the CDM (for example, order-entry applications, supplies and materials management applications, and surgery applications) should also be involved. If the CDM can be regarded as the hub of a wheel, then the various linked applications are the spokes.
- Decision Support staff (larger environments): These individuals perform report-writing and data mining. In addition, they may perform data sorts of the entire CDM computer file or certain fields within it and also may compile audit reports.

Appoint Audit Team

After these subject matter experts have determined the goal(s), scope, and frequency of the audit, the second step is to appoint members of the audit team who will conduct the actual audit.

Audit team members must have the requisite skills and knowledge to validate CDM data, so they must be selected carefully. Team members may be the stakeholders themselves, or their designees. In either case, the audit team must be aware of and accountable for the goal(s), scope, and frequency of the audit. Regarding the amount of staff, there is no one formula to set staffing levels for auditing; each organization needs to determine what amount of auditing staff is reasonable. Larger environments may employ a staff of one or more internal auditors whose job it is to conduct CDM audits. This staff is budgeted for and their work is financially supported as a part of the organization's compliance plan. Smaller organizations may not have a formal internal auditing department or staff, but must still conduct periodic CDM audits to support compliance. Adequate funds for CDM auditing should be budgeted in every annual budget cycle.

Secure Space and Equipment

The third step in CDM auditing is to secure adequate space and equipment. There should be adequate work space available for staff to perform their duties. There should be adequate lighting, heating, ventilation, and air conditioning for staff to comfortably perform their duties. Auditing is extremely detail-oriented and requires great concentration. A comfortable work environment will enhance the audit by reducing distractions such as poor lighting, leaking overhead pipes, temperatures that are too hot or cold, excessive noise, office traffic, and such. There should be adequate table or desk space. Certain reference materials will need to be accessed during the audit, some of which are available in hard-copy format only so the audit staff will likely need to spread out over a large table surface area. Certain equipment should be made available to support staff needs. Computers are essential in large environments, where the CDM may contain thousands of items. Computer hardware and software configuration should be robust enough to allow audit staff to quickly sort CDM data for review and validation.

Gather Required Supplies

The fourth step in CDM auditing is to gather certain supplies or the latest source and reference materials to support the audit as follows:

- Compliance resources: Source information is available from the Department of Health and Human Services (HHS) Office of the Inspector General (OIG) Fiscal Year Work Plan at http://www.oig.hhs.gov.
- Facility-specific compliance plan: Members of the audit team should be familiar with the details and requirements of the compliance plan.
- National Correct Coding Initiative (NCCI): A set of coding regulations to prevent fraud and abuse in physician and hospital outpatient coding.
- Coding sources and references: The Health Insurance Portability and Accountability Act (HIPAA) requires use of the following code sets, each with its own set of coding rules and conventions, which must be followed:
  - *International Classification of Diseases - 9th Revision - Clinical Modification* (ICD-9-CM) Volumes I and II, for reporting diseases and conditions
    - Source information is available online at the National Center for Health Statistics Web site (http://www.cdc.gov/nchs).

- Reference information is available in *Coding Clinic for ICD-9-CM*, published by the American Hospital Association.
- Beginning October 1, 2013, facilities will be required to submit diagnosis/condition codes using the *International Classification of Diseases - 10th Revision - Clinical Modification* (ICD-10-CM) code set.
  - *International Classification of Diseases - 9th Revision - Clinical Modification* (ICD-9-CM) Volume III, for reporting inpatient hospital procedure data
    - Source information is available online at the CMS Web site (http://www.cms.hhs.gov) and the National Center for Health Statistics Web site (http://www.cdc.gov/nchs).
    - Reference information is available in *Coding Clinic for ICD-9-CM*, published by the American Hospital Association.
    - Beginning October 1, 2013, facilities will be required to submit inpatient hospital procedure codes using the *International Classification of Diseases - 10th Revision - Procedure Classification System* (ICD-10-PCS) code set.
  - Healthcare Common Procedure Coding System (HCPCS) Level I – Current Procedural Terminology (CPT), for reporting physician and outpatient procedures and services
    - Source information is available online at the American Medical Association Web site (http://www.ama-assn.org).
    - Reference information is available in *CPT Assistant*, published by the American Medical Association, and *Coding Clinic for HCPCS*, published by the American Hospital Association.
  - Healthcare Common Procedure Coding System (HCPCS) Level II – National Codes, for reporting medical products, supplies, drugs, and other services not included in CPT
    - Source information is available online at the CMS Web site (http://www.cms.hhs.gov).
    - Reference information is available in *Coding Clinic for HCPCS*, published by the American Hospital Association.
  - *Federal Register*: Hospital Outpatient Prospective Payment System (OPPS) section, for the most current final federal rules and regulations
    - Source information is available online at http://www.gpoaccess.gov.
  - National Drug Code (NDC), for reporting drugs and biologicals
    - Source and reference information is available through the U.S. Food and Drug Administration and online at http://www.fda.gov.
- CDM vendor resources: There are hundreds of patient accounting systems on the market, and each one has its own CDM module or component. The facility's patient accounting software vendor will usually have valuable information available. The most helpful is their user's guide or manual, which spells out in detail their requirements for CDM maintenance at the CDM file and field levels.

- Determine the allowable data requirements within each field of the CDM: The data entry requirements within fields of the CDM file, known as field delimiters, vary from vendor to vendor. One field delimiter is "character type" (alphabetic, numeric, or alphanumeric). Characters entered into any field must be of the correct type. For example, CPT codes are 5-character numeric codes, thus in the CPT code field, only numeric characters are acceptable. Fortunately, many software programs have built-in error messages that alert the user to these field-level delimiters during data entry, so when one attempts to enter an alphabetic character into the CPT code field, an error message such as "numeric characters only" will appear. Another delimiter is "field width" or the number of alphabetic or numeric characters that the field can accommodate. For example, the field "charge description" may have a character limit of 25, which means that the description of any CDM charge item must be stated in 25 characters or less. In healthcare, this can be a real challenge because some medical terms have 20 or more letters (for example, esophagogastroduodenoscopy).
- National Coverage Determinations (NCDs): detail various national medical necessity and reimbursement regulations.
- Local Coverage Determinations (LCDs): detail medical necessity and reimbursement policies set by the regional fiscal intermediaries.
- Other public and private payer guidelines: detail medical necessity and reimbursement policies set by various other entities.
- The CDM file itself (hardcopy or electronic).

Conduct Audit

The fifth step is to conduct the actual review of the CDM fields, taking care to specifically validate all data elements. Members of the audit team must have the proper audit mentality, which is to strive for the utmost CDM accuracy and consistency, involving all relevant stakeholders, and using all available resources to support the compliance plan, the revenue cycle, and the organization's mission. They will need to actively coordinate and communicate throughout the audit.

The CDM is the vehicle through which a healthcare facility conducts all its charging operations. It is the link between the front-end ordering systems and the back-end billing systems. Consequently, every billable but not separately payable procedure, service, drug, or supply should be included in the CDM. Additionally, there should be reasonable expectation of coverage or payment and reimbursement for the item or service. The exception to this guideline is charge codes included in the CDM for statistical purposes. These items or services are included in the CDM for internal tracking and are not meant to be used for billing purposes.

During the audit, the audit team should ask the clinical department managers the following questions related to billing and reimbursement. For example, is every billable but not separately payable procedure, service, drug, or supply used in your department included in the CDM? An example of a billable but not separately payable supply is a patient who presents to the emergency department needing a laceration sutured. The suture supply item is setup in the CDM at $15 per suture. Suturing services are covered and billable, and although Medicare will not pay for the suture supply item, charge-based payers will. So it is important to include such items on the CDM. Another question to ask the department manager is if the staff performs any services or procedures other than those listed in the CDM. If so, the CDM committee should consider if these items should be added to the CDM. This may be a good time to discuss the established CDM workflows with the department manager.

Linked and Exploding Charge Items

Some facilities may use charging strategies known as linking charges and exploding charges. It is important that the execution of these strategies is carefully audited as improper execution can result in significant compliance issues. Linked charge items is a charging strategy typically used in ancillary department systems. For example, in the lab, the CDM item for "blood draw" is typically linked to all CDM items for lab services that require a blood draw, such as a complete blood count (CBC). After the link is established, any time a CBC is performed, the linked charge for the blood draw would automatically be added to the patient's bill along with the charge for the CBC. However, parameters need to be established so that only one blood draw is reported even though multiple blood tests may be performed.

The exploded CDM charging strategy is similar to linked strategy, except that exploded CDM items contain multiple linked CDM items. Another term for exploded CDM items is "parent/child" in which one parent CDM item is associated with multiple linked child items. In such arrangements, it is important to assure that every time a parent item is used, that **all** linked child items are used, performed, or utilized during the encounter. If even one child item is not used during a given encounter, then the parent code should not be charged and all remaining child items should be charged separately.

Department Code

It is important for the auditor to verify that the department number for a given charge item is not set up incorrectly in the CDM. This will ensure that the correct department will be charged the expense and given the revenue for the services performed. Failure to map the charge item to the right department, and therefore correct general ledger area, will result in departments being inappropriately charged and credited in the cost reporting process.

Audit Findings

The audit team must carefully validate the data within the CDM fields for every item, specifically noting any data fields that are incorrect or inconsistent. All incorrect or inconsistent data items must be reviewed with the stakeholders relevant to that specific section of the CDM (department) to:

- Confirm the error or inconsistency
- Agree on the correct data
- Agree on the time frame to make the change in the CDM (immediate, at beginning of next month or quarter, or other time)
- Obtain sign-off on the data changes and timeframe, and retain the sign-off sheets for future reference

Implementation of Changes

The sixth and final step is implementation of data element changes recommended by the completed audit and agreed upon by the stakeholders. Once the stakeholders agree on the changes that should be made and the time frame in which to make them, then those changes should be scheduled to be made in the CDM at the agreed-upon time. Typically, it is the finance department staff that does the actual data entry. The incorrect data is replaced by the correct data within the CDM (and also the order entry system as necessary), noting the date of each change. The date is important because accounts with a service date before the change date will contain the old data, and accounts with a service date after the change date will contain the new data. This will be important information during post-implementation monitoring.

After the actual CDM data has been changed, clinical department staff will continue to post charges to patient accounts as they normally would, either through an order entry system or a patient accounting and charge posting system. The corrected CDM data should appear on the patient bills from this point forward. There are several ways that facilities can monitor activities post-implementation to assure that the changes have actually been made accurately.

Post-implementation Monitoring

First, a new electronic or hard-copy CDM should be obtained. A member of the audit team should carefully review the items on the new CDM against the list of items that should have been changed to assure that the changes were made. Any items not corrected during the initial CDM data entry should be corrected immediately.

Second, random sampling of patient bills should be performed within several days of the CDM changes. The patient bills should be compared to the order entry system or the charge ticket and the patient record to assure that the charge items dropped to the bill correctly and in the correct quantities. Any errors or inconsistencies noted in the order entry, patient accounting, or CDM systems should be corrected immediately. In addition, any noted documentation deficiencies on the record should be reviewed with the clinical staff so future documentation will support the most accurate charging and billing.

Third, review claims denials received from payers to note trends or patterns. As time goes on, and with careful observation and follow-up, payment denial trends or patterns will become evident. For example, one payer's report may show several error types, such as incorrect CPT codes or invalid modifier codes or incorrect revenue codes. Of course, each claim should be corrected and resubmitted to the payer, if possible. Beyond that however, the most prevalent pattern information should be routinely shared with staff for educational purposes. In a case where most of the errors are CPT coding errors, are most of the errors made by one or two coders on staff, or is there an incorrect code within the CDM? If coding staff is making errors, retraining should be performed, with follow-up afterwards as well. If the code error is hard-coded into the CDM, the code within the CDM should be changed.

Fourth, monitor, communicate, educate, and document; then monitor, communicate, educate, and document; then monitor, communicate, educate, and document some more. All stakeholders should be involved, some to a greater extent than others, but all stakeholders should be aware, take part, and have a voice. This is the heart and life-blood of the facility's compliance plan. Facilities that monitor, communicate, educate, and document are positioned much more favorably in today's compliance world than those that do not. The monitoring, communication, education, and documentation are essential to demonstrate to the OIG, payers, the community, and other stakeholders a living, breathing compliance plan versus one that is pulled off a dusty shelf, outdated, and useless.

Determining Return on Investment (ROI)

Calculating an actual dollar amount for the return on investment (ROI) associated with CDM auditing is difficult, at best, because there are so many ways in which errors or inconsistencies can happen. For instance, our audit uncovered a price error on a CDM item, in which the item should have been priced at $15, but it was set up incorrectly at $5. If we know the number of times that item was charged in the previous year, then it is possible to calculate the impact of the error by multiplying the annual volume times the difference between the incorrect price and the correct price. If our previous year's volume was 3,000, multiplied by $10 each, then the annual impact of the pricing error is $30,000 in lost revenue. In another example, our audit uncovered a CPT coding error that was hard-coded into the CDM for a given procedure. If the reimbursement for the incorrect CPT code is $2,300 and the reimbursement for the correct CPT code is $1,000, then the payer overpaid the facility $1,300 for every time the CPT code for that CDM item dropped to a patient claim. If the audit yielded many similar examples, it would not take long for the impact to reach into the hundreds of thousands or even millions of dollars.

At the beginning of this chapter, it was mentioned that value-added auditing has a focus and a purpose; the results of which yield information that is actionable; facilitate education and communication among stakeholders; enhance an organization's overall compliance, giving it a better handle on its financial operations. The previous two examples are certainly actionable. First, the data in the price and CPT code fields of the CDM items in question need to be corrected. Second, monitoring of new patient claims associated with the two corrected CDM items is required to assure that the errors have in fact been corrected. Third, any past patient claims that have activity from either of the CDM items will need to be adjusted. If the claims errors were caught and corrected within the payer's allowable time frame for claims adjudication then a simple re-billing of those claims may be sufficient. But claims with dates of service beyond the payer time frame will likely need to be written-off. Lastly, adjustments to the departments' general ledger and budget reports will be likely. In terms of facilitating education and communication among stakeholders, these examples and all others resulting from the audit should be discussed with stakeholders and staff in detail. Corrective resources should be made available, and corrective activities should be noted, recorded, and followed up. Departmental and organizational policies and procedures should be updated. Examples should be incorporated into future staff training and orientation programs. If a facility can readily demonstrate similar actions to the OIG and to others, then they have certainly enhanced their overall compliance situation and are much more likely to have a better handle on its financial operations.

In any case, value-added CDM auditing should always yield two significant results:

1. A favorable (downward or reduced) trend in delayed and denied claims
2. Increased stakeholder ownership over their part of the organization's overall compliance plan

Other likely outcomes include:

1. A favorable (downward or reduced) trend in overpayments
2. A favorable (downward or reduced) trend in underpayments
3. Improved charge capture (fewer missed charges)
4. Fewer and lower fines and penalties
5. An overall improvement in the organizations compliance standing, situation, and readiness
6. A wealth of information that can be used for staff education and training

External Audits

Voluntarily and actively participating in external auditing activities is yet another way the organization can demonstrate its compliance commitment. As such, external auditing is equally important to an organization's compliance as is internal auditing. But while internal auditing is never optional, external auditing is. The main value of external auditing is that it is another unbiased set of eyes and ears examining the charging, billing, revenue cycle, claims management, and compliance activities of the organization.

There are several benefits to bringing in external auditors. First, as mentioned previously, it is yet another way the organization can demonstrate its compliance commitment. Second, most external auditors have auditing experience in organizations spanning the entire healthcare continuum, from home health agencies to long-term care facilities, to small- and medium-sized community hospitals, to large integrated delivery networks. This broader range of experience often provides external auditors an excellent platform from which to base compliance improvement recommendations. Third, most external auditing firms can bring resources that may not be readily available to many smaller healthcare facilities, such as automated CDM-analyzer software and other computer applications. Fourth, because of their experience and resources, many external auditing engagements run for only a short time. Lastly, external audit staff are perhaps more unbiased since they are not direct employees of the organization.

However, there are several potential drawbacks with external auditing. One is that the services can be expensive. Because most external auditing firms employ well-trained and experienced staff who use the latest (and expensive) resources, their fees can be high. Second, since their staff are not employees of the organization, it is necessary to contract with the firm. Deciding on one of the many hundreds of firms out there, and then hammering-out the details of the specific contract or engagement can be time-consuming and sometimes overwhelming. Third, just because an organization contracts with an external auditing firm does not absolve it from the responsibility for an effective compliance plan—the organization is still responsible for taking effective action based on the external audit findings and recommendations.

Managing the Engagement

Hiring or engaging an external audit firm begins and ends with the contract. Contract details for external compliance auditing should include the same important considerations as with internal auditing and should contain at a minimum the following elements:

- Goal: What are the overall goals of the engagement?
- Scope: Is the engagement to be broad in scope, looking at all aspects of the organization's compliance plan? Or is the engagement to be targeted or limited,

for example to just the CDM and its feeder applications, such as order-entry, surgery, or supplies management applications?

- Term of engagement: How long will the engagement run? One year? Six months? Three months?
- Deliverables: What are the specific results desired? There may be several or many items listed here. Be very specific. The external auditing firm is responsible for making sure that they deliver these results. Perhaps the most common deliverable for these types of engagements is a set of one or more recommendations, which the organization is ultimately responsible for validating and implementing.
- Staff: Both the organization and the external auditing firm should name a point person of authority who is their main contact throughout the engagement. They would be responsible for effective coordination and communication throughout the term of the engagement. All other key stakeholders and participants should be listed, along with their contact information.
- Space: Where will the actual work be performed? Is adequate on-site work space available? How will suitable workspace be allocated and under what conditions?
- Equipment: Will the external auditors have access to the organization's on-site equipment, and if so, what equipment and under what conditions? Copiers, computers, and printers? Telephones and faxes? Network access, temporary UserIDs, and Passwords?
- Supplies: What hard-copy, electronic, or Web-based reference materials are available? Who will provide those and under what conditions?
- Fees and Costs: What fees are going to be charged by the auditing firm? Be specific here. The organization is responsible for paying these fees in full and on time. Typically, the broader the scope and the longer the term, the more expensive the engagement will likely be.
- Payment terms: The length of time allowed to pay the fees in full should be clearly delineated.
- Penalties: Are there any penalties (payment amounts) for nonperformance:
  - If the external auditing firm fails to deliver on the results expected?
  - If the organization fails to pay in full and on time?

After the external auditing firm is engaged by contract, and when the actual audit work is completed, the organization is typically left with a set of one or more written recommendations. The organization must marshal its internal subject matter experts and validate each recommendation as reasonable and accurate. For the recommendation(s) that are deemed as unreasonable or inaccurate, the organization should document its rationale, share it with the external auditing firm, and then not implement the recommendation(s). But for the recommendation(s) that the organization deems as reasonable and accurate, this is a critical time for the organization—"where the rubber hits the road"—because it is these recommendation(s) that the organization should implement. Most organizations do, and as a result, they improve their compliance situation and readiness. But some do not, and these organizations put their compliance standing in serious jeopardy.

Implementing Recommendations

As with internal audits, armed with a set of written recommendations from an external auditing engagement, the organization's internal stakeholders should agree and sign off on the manner and time frame in which internal changes are to be made. Those internal changes should be scheduled to be made in the manner and time frame established. Every change should be made, and each should be clearly documented, whether it is a data change in the CDM, a change in a policy or procedure, a change to a computer interface between two systems, or any other. It is this very documentation that clearly demonstrates that the organization is serious about compliance—it shows that it actually takes definitive action to support and improve their compliance situation and readiness.

After the actual changes have been made, and as with internal audits, facilities must monitor activities post-implementation to ensure that the changes have been made accurately. The same internal monitoring methods are used as with internal audits: random sampling of patient claims should continue regularly—claims should be compared to the order entry system, charge ticket, or superbill and to the patient record to guarantee accuracy; documentation deficiencies on the record should be reviewed with the clinical staff; claims denials should be reviewed to note trends or patterns; and monitor, communicate, educate, and document. Again, this is the heart and lifeblood of the facility's compliance plan. Facilities that monitor, communicate, educate, and document are positioned much more favorably in today's compliance world than those that do not.

References

Institute of Internal Auditors. 2010. http://www.theiia.org.

Roth, J. 2003. How do internal auditors add value? Characteristics common to top-rated audit shops help to shed light on the nebulous concept of adding value. http://findarticles.com/p/articles/mi_m4153/is_1_60/ai_98009241/.

Resources

American Health Information Management Association. 1999. Practice brief: The care and maintenance of charge masters. *Journal of AHIMA* 70(7):80A–B.

Casto, A. and E. Layman. 2009. *Principles of Healthcare Reimbursement*, 2nd ed. Chicago: AHIMA.

Drach, M. 2001 (January). Ten steps to successful chargemaster reviews. *Journal of AHIMA* 72(1):42–48.

Chapter 8

Pricing

Susan White, PhD, CHDA

For the purposes of this chapter, the terms "price" and "charge" will be treated as synonymous. The term "cost" refers to the actual cost incurred by the provider when dispensing the item or service.

The charge description master (CDM) houses the price for each item dispensed by a healthcare entity. Ensuring that the current price for each line item is accurately reflected in the CDM should be a part of periodic CDM maintenance. The prices for new CDM items may be required on an ad hoc basis. The task of actually selecting the price for an item is often completed by the Finance department, an interdisciplinary pricing team, or it is outsourced to a consulting firm. Pricing may be performed as a component of a complete CDM review or as a stand-alone project. It is best practice to ensure that the CDM is accurate and complete prior to commencing a pricing project.

The prices in a CDM may be updated for a number of reasons. One consideration may be changes in the cost to deliver a service. There are a number of services that may have little or no change in cost to deliver from year to year. The prices for these services should be updated to reflect losses that may be attributed to governmental payers, amounts written off due to self-pay patients, and the need for the facility to make a reasonable margin on the entire collection of services provided.

The key to a successful pricing project is good communication between the CDM and finance teams. The CDM team may be in the best position to assess the practical aspects of the prices. For instance, the CDM team should make the pricing team aware of any codes that are priced zero by design. CDMs often contain codes that are used for statistical purposes and never appear as a charge on a bill. If that information is not shared among all users of the CDM, then prices may be assigned that could result in potential compliance issues. Similarly, line item additions and deletions should be communicated to the pricing team. The revenue from deleted items was likely built into the current budget and must be reallocated to items remaining in the CDM.

Prices for pharmacy services are often maintained in the pharmacy system or CDM and are not typically part of the pricing methodology used for other facility services. The pricing of pharmacy services is typically based on a markup or multiplier of cost. The cost used as a basis for the price may be an average cost over a period of time or may be based on the actual invoice from the purchase of the pharmaceutical. The accurate transfer of prices from the pharmacy system to the facility billing system is often a challenge due to differences in dose dispensed and dose description for appropriate HCPCS Level II codes. This chapter will not address the maintenance issues associated with the pharmacy portion of the CDM.

Prior to discussing pricing strategies, it is important to understand the scrutiny that healthcare prices are now under. The price for healthcare services is no longer a closely guarded secret. Consumers, government entities, and health plans are all giving more attention to the reasonableness and comparability of pricing. The activity around publically releasing pricing is a part of a larger movement for healthcare transparency.

Price Transparency

The charge for healthcare services is under far more scrutiny as the number of participants in high-deductible (HSA-compatible) health plans increases. Prior to the development of these plans, only the provider and third party payers were interested in the comparison of charges between providers. However, if a patient is covered under a health plan with a $2,500 deductible and must decide where to go for an MRI, that patient is motivated to shop around and compare prices at the various provider options. A similar patient with a traditional health plan may simply go to the closest radiology center or the hospital with which their physician is associated.

The Commonwealth Fund published a report on healthcare transparency. The authors outlined three important reasons for transparency:

1. To help providers improve by benchmarking their performance against others
2. To encourage private insurers and public programs to reward quality and efficiency
3. To help patients make informed choices about their care (Collins 2006)

In April 2006, the American Hospital Association Board of Directors approved a resolution that included the goals and objectives for price transparency as well as a road map to price transparency. These goals and objectives of this resolution are displayed in figure 8.1.

Goal:
Share meaningful information with consumers about the price of their hospital care

Objectives:
- Present information in a way that is easy for consumers to understand and use
- Make information easy for consumers to access
- Create common definitions and language to describe pricing information for consumers
- Explain to consumers how and why the price of their care can vary
- Encourage consumers to include price information as just one of several considerations in making healthcare decisions
- Direct consumers to additional information about financial assistance with their hospital care

---

Source: AHA 2006.

Figure 8.1.   AHA Resolution, April 2006

The Challenge

The concept of presenting price or charge information for healthcare services to potential patients seems relatively simple. Unfortunately, purchasing healthcare is not like purchasing an automobile or ordering dinner at a restaurant. There is a menu (the Chargemaster), but it is the physician that orders on behalf of the patients and not the patients themselves. For instance, a physician may inform a patient that he or she will have an MRI to try to diagnose the source of chronic back pain. Suppose this is the patient used as an example above with a $2,500 deductible HAS-compatible health plan. The patient may search for comparative prices for local providers by searching the Internet or calling providers with a price inquiry. The challenge is how to assist the patient in getting an accurate price for the service that will be ordered by the physician. If the patient simply asks for the provider's charge for an MRI, they may receive a misleading answer. The following information would help refine the price question:

- What body part will be imaged?
- Will contrast be used? If so, how much contrast?
- Will this be a single image or one with and one without contrast?

Of course, the most accurate price will be obtained by stating the actual CPT procedure code that will be performed. This MRI example is likely one of the simpler outpatient examples. Imagine asking a provider for the price of a cardiac catheterization? The number of variables that may determine the price of that service is astronomical.

Careoperatives, LLC carried out a study to determine how difficult it would be for a patient to obtain pricing information for an anterior cruciate ligament (ACL) repair of the knee. Their researchers were much more successful in obtaining prices from ambulatory surgery centers (ASC) than hospitals. Since ASCs have historically been paid via a case rate (ASC Groups), it is not surprising that they are set up to bill and

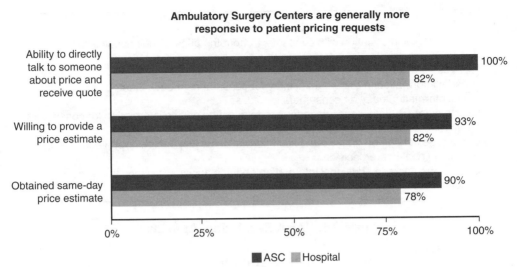

Figure 8.2.   Experience in obtaining a price quote for ACL repair

quote on a case basis. Hospitals, on the other hand, are more likely paid on a procedure basis either via fee schedules, Ambulatory Patient Classifications (APCs) or a percent of charge basis. In order to be properly paid under these systems, each component of the service must be charged separately.

On average, it required three times more phone calls to obtain a price from a hospital versus an ASC. The length of each call was four times longer for the hospital setting. The researchers also found that 70 percent of hospitals would not guarantee the price. Many hospital representatives would only supply price ranges and some were very wide. The data displayed in figure 8.2 shows that ASCs were more responsive to pricing inquiries (Careoperatives 2010).

Obviously, there is a struggle between the desire to share pricing information and the difficultly in sharing it in a format that is useful to patients and health plans. A number of states have passed or are contemplating legislation to require the release of some level of hospital pricing information. In the next section, we will review some of the strategies that have been implemented to date.

Strategies for Public Release of Pricing Information

To answer this call for more information from consumers, a number of states have comparative pricing data available online either through a government-supported site or one maintained by the state hospital association. Each of the implementations has different levels of detail and requirements for data submission. Some examples of state pricing databases are listed in table 8.1.

Table 8.1.   Examples of publically available hospital price comparisons

State	Organization Maintaining Information	Web site Link	Scope of Data Available
Wisconsin	Wisconsin Hospital Association	http://www.wipricepoint.org/	Inpatient, outpatient, emergency services
Washington	Washington State Hospital Association	http://www.wahospitalpricing.org/	Inpatient services by MS-DRG
Texas	Texas Hospital Association	http://www.txpricepoint.org/	Inpatient services by MS-DRG
California	Office of Statewide Health Planning and Development	http://www.oshpd.ca.gov/ Chargemaster/	CDM level detail

The prices set for hospital services are often difficult to provide to consumers. The databases typically take the user down a path of querying with increased specificity. For instance, to make an inpatient price comparison, it will typically lead the user down the path depicted in figure 8.3. This strategy works well from the implementation side since each claim will be assigned to one unique MS-DRG. Unfortunately, the typical consumer does not actually think in terms of major diagnostic categories (MDCs) and may not know in what body system their ailment existed.

Queries for obtaining comparative pricing for outpatient services are not as straightforward. There is no claim grouping that will uniquely identify a hospital outpatient service. A claim may have more than one Ambulatory Payment Classification (APC).

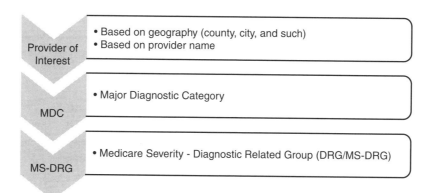

Figure 8.3.   Typical user path for hospital inpatient price comparisons

Ambulatory Payment Groups (APGs) are not widely implemented. The strategy implemented by the Wisconsin Hospital Association takes the user down the path of selecting the setting (emergency or outpatient), the provider, a diagnosis category (body part, minor injuries, or infections) and finally produces a summary based on a range of ICD-9-CM diagnosis codes. The Wisconsin Hospital Association price comparison database is located at http://www.wipricepoint.org.

In California, each hospital is required to submit a copy of their Chargemaster to the Office of Statewide Health Planning and Development. This strategy results in one of the most comprehensive databases of prices available, but it is not user-friendly. In addition to the complete Chargemaster, each hospital must also submit the prices for a set of 25 common outpatient procedures. California law also requires hospitals to provide a price estimate to uninsured patients and then collect the amount that a government payer would reimburse the hospital (Farrell 2010, 110). Researchers studied the effectiveness of this policy and found that only 28 percent of hospitals responded with price estimates and 75 percent of those estimates exceeded the Medicare reimbursement for the procedures.

We do not have true price transparency in the healthcare market at this time. Purchasing healthcare is not like purchasing an automobile or ordering dinner, but the amount of pricing information available to consumers has evolved quickly and will continue to evolve. Price transparency is a deceptively simple concept that is proving to be difficult to implement. The single most important point that providers should take from these forays into full price disclosure is that hospital prices are no longer considered a trade secret and must be formulated using a defensible strategy.

Strategies for Price Setting

Although the CDM team typically does not set prices, the team should be aware of the facility's price setting strategy. It is important for the CDM team to understand how prices are set and the time required for research and price setting. Having a good understanding of the price setting strategy will help the CDM team to see the big picture or overall financial strategy of the healthcare facility.

Facilities use a range of methodologies in updating prices. Updating prices could be as simple as applying a uniform percent increase to every item or a set of items in the CDM. This pricing methodology is often called an across-the-board or ATB price adjustment. Although it is the most simple of all pricing strategies, it often does not yield the best net revenue return since it ignores patient mix for each service. Pricing may also be based solely on the net income impact or profitability of each price change. Most pricing teams use a blend of methodologies that take the following three critical components into consideration:

1. Net income requirements
2. Market position
3. Defensibility

No matter which strategy a facility decides to use, the change in prices for any item in the CDM will have an impact on both the gross and net revenue of the facility. As an illustration, consider the following example.

Suppose the price for CPT 80047 – Basic Metabolic Panel is currently $15 at Sample Hospital. We know from the revenue and usage report that the facility performed 10,000 of these tests last year. If we increase the price of the test by 10 percent to $16.50, then the gross revenue for that test will increase from $150,000 to $165,000. If Sample Hospital has only one payer and this payer pays 75 percent of charges for laboratory services, then the corresponding increase in net revenue will be from $112,500 (75 percent of $150,000) to $123,750 (75 percent of $165,000). In this relatively simple example, the 10 percent increase in gross revenue yields an equivalent 10 percent increase in net revenue.

The example above is not very realistic. Very few facilities are reimbursed based on a percentage of charge by all of their payers. Typically, there is a mix of reimbursement methodologies for each service that is dependent on the mix of setting (inpatient, out-patient, emergency) where the service is provided and payment terms appropriate for that patient. In order to truly assess the impact on net revenue of any pricing strategy, the facility must be able to accurately model the expected payment for each service under various pricing scenarios.

Net Income Requirements

One of the drivers of a healthcare facility's annual budget is the net income derived from price changes. Net income is the cost to provide a service subtracted from the payment. Net income may also be referred to as profit. Strategic price increases and decreases can improve a facility's profitability while limiting the overall change in gross revenue. The volume and payer mix for a service may be used to determine its optimal price. The payer mix will determine the net revenue price sensitivity or recovery rate for a service. The percentage of a price change that is realized by a facility as a change in net revenue or reimbursement is sometimes called the recovery rate. The recovery rate for any item in the CDM may range from 0 to 1. For instance, if a lab procedure were paid at 75 percent of charges, then the recovery rate would be 0.75. The facility will net 75 cents for each one dollar increase in price for that procedure.

Many payer contracts include a provision that sets the payment to be the lesser of the charge and the fee schedule or case rate. The pricing team should be aware of the services that are impacted by this type of contract provision. Generally, the pricing team should strive to price those items and services above the fee schedule or case rate to ensure that the payment amount is not decreased to the charges. Setting the prices for case rates that involve many CDM items requires careful analysis of the items typically billed during those cases. The recovery rate for these items is one up to the fee schedule amount. That is, the increase in payment for every dollar increase in price is one to one up to the fee schedule amount. The recovery rate would be zero once the price exceeds the payment level.

If all payers reimburse for a procedure via a fee schedule with no provision to accept the less of charges or the fee, then the recovery rate for that item would be zero. The formula for calculating the recovery rate is shown in table 8.2. The price of the service has no impact on the net revenue for the service, since any increase in price would yield no incremental increase in payment. Conversely, if all payers reimburse at a rate of 100 percent of charges for that same procedure, then the recovery rate would be 1. If all payers reimburse at a rate of 75 percent of charges, the recovery rate would be 0.75. For every dollar the price is increased, the provider will take in 75 cents more in net revenue or payment. Each service in a typical Chargemaster will have a distinct payer mix and therefore a distinct recovery rate. By strategically choosing which prices to increase or decrease, the net income derived from a set of prices can be optimized.

Again we refer to our lab test example, 80047 – Basic Metabolic Panel, but this time we will make the situation a bit more realistic. The facility typically performs 10,000 of these tests per year and the current price is $15. Assume that the payer mix for this procedure is represented in table 8.3.

Table 8.2.   Example Recovery Rate Calculation – CPT 71020 (chest x-ray)

Payer	Contract Term	Volume	Payment at Original Price ($125)	Payment at New Price ($126)	Change in payment due to $1 price increase	Payer-Specific Recovery Rate
HMO 1	Fee Schedule Payment = $20	100	$20.00	$20.00	$0.00	0
PPO	Percent of charge = 65%	190	$81.25	$81.90	0.65	65%
Item Recovery Rate						42.6%

Note: Item Recovery Rate = [(100×0)+(190×.65)]/(100+190)

Table 8.3.   Payer Mix for CPT 80047

Payer	Payment Terms for 80047	Recovery Rate	Annual Volume of 80047
Medicare	Fee Schedule	0.00	3,300
Commercial Contract 1	Percent of Charge 75%	0.75	4,500
HMO A	Fee Schedule	0.00	2,200
Total		0.34	10,000

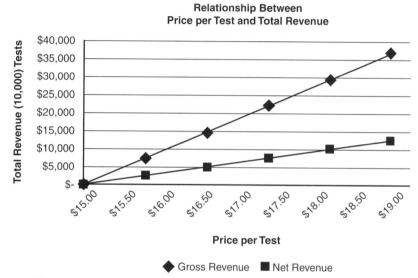

Figure 8.4.   Relationship between Price and Total Revenue

The recovery rate for CPT 80047 would then be the weighted average of the individual payer recovery rates for the procedure or 34 percent (3300*(0.00) + 4500*(0.75) + 2200*(0) = 0.34). This means that for every dollar increase in price, the facility will take in thirty-four cents in net revenue. If we assume that the net income requirement for this procedure was an additional $7,000, then the price must be set so that the provider will receive an additional 70 cents ($7,000/10,000 tests) per test. In order to achieve the additional 70 cents in net revenue per test, we must increase the price for the procedure by 0.7/0.34 or $2.06. A price of $17.06 will allow the provider to meet the required net income for this test. Since the net income for a service is also a function of the cost to provide the service, the underlying assumption here is that the cost to produce the test remains relatively constant from year to year.

Figure 8.4 demonstrates the dramatic difference in the change in gross and net revenue as the price for the example test increases. Understanding this relationship is critical when balancing the net income requirements from a price adjustment with the other two critical factors—market position and defensibility.

Market Position

It is important to understand a facility's market position prior to commencing a pricing project. The market should be analyzed to assess two critical questions:

1. How does the facility's prices compare to local and regional peers'?
2. What market share does the facility current capture?

There are a number of strategies for acquiring the data necessary to make a comparison to peer hospitals or peer groups. The Price Transparency section of this chapter lists a number of resources to obtain comparative prices at the CPT code or MS-DRG level. A number of vendors also offer comparative pricing data that is typically derived from the Medicare claims databases that CMS distributes. Comparative pricing at the CDM line item level is far more difficult to acquire. Each facility's CDM charge identifier codes are unique to its set of services. The exception to this would be facilities that are part of a larger system that may have a standard CDM. These facilities would have the opportunity to benchmark their prices within the system, but would still not be able to make global comparisons to peers outside of the system.

In practice APC, CPT, HCPCS, and MS-DRG level pricing is the most common form of price comparisons. More refined inpatient comparisons may be made by comparing charge by revenue code or department. The individual item code that is causing a variance may not be immediately identified, but that type of comparison will certainly help point the analyst to the correct department or even revenue code.

Defensibility

Facility rate changes often become public knowledge either through required disclosures or press inquiries. Now, more than ever, it is critical that price changes are defensible. There are three primary questions that providers ask in defending their prices:

1. How do my prices compare to my peers'?
2. Are my prices aligned with the resources required to deliver the service?
3. Is my overall facility profitability comparable to the industry norms?

Peer comparisons at the procedure or inpatient admission level are available from a number of commercial and government sources. In states where public disclosure of pricing data is not required, Medicare data is available to perform price benchmarking for most procedures.

The relative cost of two procedures is typically estimated via use of a cost accounting system. Care must be taken to ensure that both the direct and indirect costs of providing the service are taken into consideration. For example, the cost of the materials to perform a laboratory test may be $5 per test. There are a number of other direct fixed costs that must be considered: the salary and benefits of the laboratory staff, the cost of maintaining the laboratory and its equipment, the cost of leasing or buying the equipment, and such. A number of indirect or overhead costs must also be allocated to the test: the cost of registering patients for the test, the cost of generating a claim, the cost of collecting payment for the test, and such. All of these costs must be considered when setting and defending the price of a service.

There are some situations where a facility may price two services with the same CPT or HCPCS code differently. If the cost to provide the service is different, then this practice is defensible. Consider the situation where a laboratory test is provided to both patients at the facility and when the facility is acting as a reference laboratory processing specimens that may be collected at another site. In this case, the amount of resources consumed when performing the test is different. The amount of resources expended when performing the test as a reference laboratory may have a lower indirect cost rate. This service should be assigned its own CDM item code and may have a lower price.

Hospital profitability may be measured by comparing a facility's overall margin to external standards. The Medicare Payment Advisory Commission (MedPAC) Data Book is released on an annual basis and contains a number of valuable facility level benchmarking statistics. MedPAC was established as an independent government agency by the Balanced Budget Act of 1997. It was formulated to advise Congress on healthcare payment and quality issues for both the Medicare and private payer patients. The Data

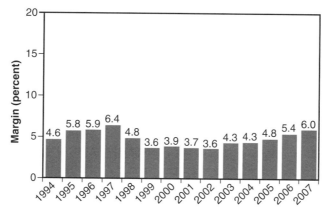

Note: A margin is calculated as revenue minus costs, divided by revenue. Total margin includes all patient care services funded by all payers, plus nonpatient revenue. Analysis excludes critical access hospitals.

Source: MedPAC 2009.

Figure 8.5.   MedPAC margin statistics

Book is released in June of each year. Figure 8.5 is an example of the data available in this publication. Hospital margins are also tabulated by urban or rural setting, teaching level, and other facility demographic variables (MedPAC 2009).

When providing data to defend pricing structure, benchmarking against a government source or other third party measures can lend credibility to the analysis. There are a number of consulting firms that provide customized studies that can provide support for a facility's pricing structure. They may be found by searching the Internet or by referring to the Healthcare Financial Management Association's (HFMA) vendor listings.

Summary

The pricing of services for healthcare entities can be a complex project. According to a survey performed in December 2005 by the Lewin Group on behalf of MedPAC, less than one third of hospitals implemented uniform or across-the-board price increases. (Dobson 2005,19) This survey also asked hospital administrators to rate a number of factors that influence their pricing strategies on a 5-point Likert Scale (1 = not important, to 5 = highly important). Table 8.4 summarizes the results.

It is interesting to note that cost considerations and hospital mission topped the list. Hospital Mission is essentially related to the defensibility issue of maintaining a reasonable margin. Since seven of the eight factors are separated by only 0.5 points on the rating scale, hospital executives believe that pricing is a bit of a balancing act.

Poorly thought out price decreases could leave a facility with a price that is under the cost to produce the service. An unreasonable price increase could leave the facility in a better financial position but cause a public relations nightmare. A successful pricing

Table 8.4.   Factors Influencing Pricing

Chargemaster Influencing Factor	Mean (n = 57)
Overall Cost Inflation	3.89
Changes in Costs of Specific Services, Procedures, and Devices	3.75
Hospital Mission	3.74
Competitive Forces	3.67
Influence of Specific Payers	3.65
Community Perception	3.44
Managed Care Contract Terms	3.31
Indirect Cost Allocation	2.43

Source: Collins and Davis 2006; Dobson 2005.

strategy is a balancing act that requires careful analysis of each price change to ensure that there are no unintended consequences.

References

American Hospital Association. 2006. Hospital pricing transparency. http://www.aha.org/aha/content/2006/pdf/5_1_06_sb_transparency.pdf.

Careoperatives, LLC. 2010. Surgery secrets: The challenges patients face. White paper. *Healthcare Blue Book.* http://healthcarebluebook.com/PDF_Files/100203%20HCBB%20White%20Paper%20-Surgery%20Pricing%20Secrets.pdf.

Collins, S.R. and K. Davis. 2006. Transparency in health care: The time has come. *The Commonwealth Fund.* http://www.commonwealthfund.org/usr_doc/TransparencyTestimony_Collins_3-15-06.pdf.

Dobson, A. 2005. *A Study of Hospital Charge Setting Practices.* Washington, D.C.: Lewin Group.

Farrell, K. S., L. J. Finocchio, A. N. Trivedi, and A. Mehrotra. 2010. Does price transparency legislation allow the unsured to shop for care? *Journal of General Internal Medicine* 25(2):110–114.

Medicare Payment Advisory Commission. 2009. Data book: Healthcare spending and the medicare program. http://www.medpac.gov/documents/jun09databookentirereport.pdf.

Chapter 9

Managing High-Risk Areas

Anne B. Casto, RHIA, CCS

M anaging the CDM is a complex process as we have discussed throughout this text. In this chapter we will discuss areas that tend to be high-risk areas for several facilities. Areas can be high risk for different reasons. The areas could have complex compliance issues or have a significant impact to reimbursement if not properly executed. No matter what the reason, the following areas should be given adequate attention to ensure proper reporting of services to produce an accurate and complete claim.

Pharmacy CDM

The location of pharmacy line items varies from facility to facility. At some hospitals the pharmacy line items may be housed in the main CDM; other hospitals may choose to have a separate CDM. If there is a separate pharmacy CDM, then some hospitals interface the pharmacy charges to the main CDM and then to the patient accounting system. Others will have the pharmacy CDM interface directly to the patient accounting system. Figure 9.1 shows different models that are utilized for CDM and pharmacy CDM structure.

The pharmacy area is a complex component of the CDM because two code sets are used by the facility to track pharmacy items and the dosage must be closely monitored. HCPCS Level II codes are the designated code set for reporting drugs on the claim form. However, the Pharmacy department also maintains the National Drug Code (NDC) numbers as these are the codes used for purchasing drugs from the manufacturer. Therefore, there is typically an additional column in the pharmacy CDM to record the NDC. This becomes complex as there can be a many NDC codes and a single or few HCPCS codes as shown in table 9.1. Please note: Be careful with this acronym as to not confuse NDC (national drug code) with NCD (national coverage determination).

As you can see in table 9.1, drugs are produced in multiple doses and in some instances by multiple manufacturers; the NDC structure allows for both of these issues. How-

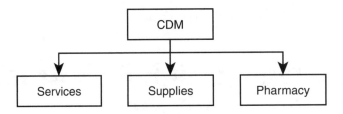

Pharmacy line items included in CDM

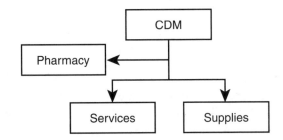

Separate Pharmacy CDM without interface into CDM

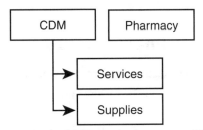

Figure 9.1.   Various CDM and pharmacy CDM models

ever, the HCPCS Level II codes typically allow for one code per drug and have one set dosage amount. Therefore, the pharmacy line items must be structured very carefully so that the correct unit of service is reported on the claim. For example, consider the administration of Zofran prior to ambulatory surgery. Four milligrams of Zofran is administered to the patient via an IV injection. For the pharmacy this may be one unit of 00173-0442. But for claim reporting, code J2405 should be reported with four units of service. In order to convert NDC units to HCPCS Level II units, facilities assign a multiplier to the pharmacy line item as shown in figure 9.2. The Pharmacy department and CDM team must work together to ensure that the multipliers are accurate. CMS may change the dosage unit in the HCPCS Level II code book during the annual updates. Though this does not happen very often, the CDM team must review the J-codes very closely each year. Failing to address a dosage unit change can result in either an underpayment or overpayment to the facility.

Table 9.1. NDC and HCPCS Level II Code Listing for Zofran

Zofran Injection Codes					
NDC Code	**Description**	**Strength**	**HCPCS Code**	**Description**	**Unit**
55154-1112	Zofran Solution for Injection	2MG/ML	J2405	Injection, ondansetron HCl, up to 1 MG	1MG
51947-8211	Zofran Injection Solution	4MG/ML			
00173-0461	Zofran Injection Premixed	32 MG/50ML			
00173-0442	Zofran Injection Solution	4MG/2ML			
00409-8253	Zofran Injection Premixed Ondansetron Hydrochloride	32MG			
Zofran Oral Solution Codes					
NDC Code	**Description**	**Strength**	**HCPCS Code**	**Description**	**Unit**
00173-0489	Zofran Oral Solution	4MG/5ML	Q0179	Ondansetron HCl, oral, 8 MG (under special Medicare circumstances only)	8MG
53873-0489	Zofran Oral Solution	4MG/5ML	S0181	Ondansetron HCl, oral, 4 MG (non-Medicare code)	4MG
Zofran Tablets Codes					
NDC Code	**Description**	**Strength**	**HCPCS Code**	**Description**	**Unit**
12634*871	Zofran Tablets	8MG	Q0179	Ondansetron HCl, oral, 8 MG (under special Medicare circumstances only)	8MG
55154-1121	Zofran Tablets	8MG	S0181	Ondansetron HCl, oral, 4 MG (non-Medicare code)	4MG

Continued

Table 9.1.   NDC and HCPCS Level II Code Listing for Zofran *(Continued)*

| Zofran Injection Codes | | | | | |
NDC Code	Description	Strength	HCPCS Code	Description	Unit
55154-1132	Zofran ODT Tablets	4MG			
62938-0501	Zofran ODT Tablets	4MG			
62938-0502	Zofran ODT Tablets	8MG			
00173-0447	Zofran Tablets Film Coated	8MG			
00173-0570	Zofran ODT Tablets	8MG			
00173-0446	Zofran Tablets Film Coated	4MG			
00173-0569	Zofran ODT Tablets	4MG			
53873-0447	Zofran Tablets	8MG			
53873-0570	Zofran ODT Tablets	8MG			
53873-0569	Zofran ODT Tablets	4MG			
53873-0446	Zofran Tablets	4MG			
49999-*783	Zofran Tablets	8MG			
51129-1530	Zofran Tablets	8MG			
51129-1531	Zofran Tablets	4MG			
68071-*057	Zofran ODT Tablets	4MG			
54868-5089	Zofran ODT Tablets	8MG			
54868-3509	Zofran Tablets	8MG			
54868-3508	Zofran Tablets	4MG			
58016-*084	Zofran Tablets	8MG			
58016-*826	Zofran Tablets	4MG			
58016-*602	Zofran ODT Tablets	4MG			

*Zofran is brand name
Source: FDA 2010;CMS 2010a.

```
NDC unit * multiplier = HCPCS unit
00173-0442 * 4 = 4
```

Figure 9.2.   Pharmacy CDM multiplier

Another issue that the pharmacy and CDM team must consider is the dispensing unit versus the HCPCS Level II unit and how the facility handles waste allowances. There should be a policy and procedure to address drug waste. The policy and procedure may or may not be payer specific. For example, consider the administration of Zofran prior to ambulatory surgery again. However, this time six milligrams of Zofran is administered to the patient via an IV injection. For the pharmacy this may be two units of 00173-0442. But for claim reporting, code J2405 should be reported with six units of service. What happens to the other 22 milligrams of Zofran? See Figure 9.3. The determination is based on whether the drug is provided in a single-use vial or package versus a multiple-use vial or package. The pharmacy unit must ensure its waste units are reported only when allowed by the payer to ensure that overpayments are not received by the facility.

You can search for NDCs online via the U.S. Food and Drug Administration Web site at http://www.accessdata.fda.gov/scripts/cder/ndc/default.cfm.

Self-Administered Drugs

Self-administered drugs can be a tricky area for CDM teams because some payers, such as state workers compensation, will cover self-administered drugs and others, like Medicare, have excluded them from the benefit plan. It is important for CDM teams to be up to date on self-administered drug reporting requirements for Medicare. The Medicare Benefit Policy Manual (Pub 100-02 of Internet-Only Manuals) Chapter 15, Section 50.2 provides definitions and guidance for self-administered drugs under Medicare.

According to Medicare, a self-administered drug is one in which the medication is self-administered by the Medicare beneficiary more than 50 percent of the time for all Medicare beneficiaries who use the drug (CMS 2010c). The determination is not made on a beneficiary-by-beneficiary basis, but rather on a drug-by-drug basis. Medicare Administrative Contractors must publish on their Web site the process they use to determine if a drug is usually self-administered and therefore does not meet the "incident to" benefit category. Additionally, they must provide a list of injectable self-administered drugs that are subject to the self-administered exclusion. Contractors must also enter their self-administration drug exclusion list to the Medicare Coverage Database, which can be accessed at http://www.cms.hhs.gov/mcd.

40 - Discarded Drugs and Biologicals
(Rev. 1478, Issued: 03-14-08 Effective: 01-01-08; Implementation: 04-14-08)

The CMS encourages physicians, hospitals and other providers to schedule patients in such a way that they can use drugs or biologicals most efficiently, in a clinically appropriate manner. However, if a physician, hospital or other provider must discard the remainder of a single use vial or other single use package after administering a dose/quantity of the drug or biological to a Medicare patient, the program provides payment for the amount of drug or biological discarded along with the amount administered, up to the amount of the drug or biological as indicated on the vial or package label.

When processing all drugs except those provided under the Competitive Acquisition Program for Part B drugs and biologicals (CAP), local contractors may require the use of the modifier JW to identify unused drug or biologicals from single use vials or single use packages that are appropriately discarded. This modifier will provide payment for the discarded drug or biological. The JW modifier is not used on claims for CAP drugs.

For CAP drugs, please see subsection 100.2.9 - Submission of Claims With the Modifier JW, "Drug or Biological Amount Discarded/Not Administered to Any Patient", for additional discussion of the discarded remainder of a vial or other packaged drug or biological in the CAP. **NOTE:** Multi-use vials are not subject to payment for discarded amounts of drug or biological.

EXAMPLE 1:

A provider schedules three Medicare patients to receive Botulinum Toxin Type A on the same day within the designated shelf life of the product. Currently, Botox is available only in a 100-unit size. Once Botox is reconstituted, it has a shelf life of only four hours. Often, a patient receives less than a 100 unit dose. The provider administers 30 units to each of the three patients. The remaining 10 units that must be discarded are billed to Medicare on the account of the last patient. Therefore, 30 units are billed on behalf of the first patient seen and 30 units are billed on behalf of the second patient seen. Forty units are billed on behalf of the last patient seen because the provider had to discard 10 units at that point.

EXAMPLE 2:

A provider administers 15 units of Botulinum Toxin Type A to a Medicare patient, and it is not practical to schedule another patient who requires Botulinum Toxin. The remaining 85 units are discarded. For example, the provider may have only one patient who requires Botulinum Toxin, or the patient requiring treatment may be previously unknown to the provider, thereby precluding consideration of the treatment modality in scheduling the new patient. The provider bills for 100 units on behalf of the patient and Medicare pays for 100 units.

Source: CMS 2010b.
Figure 9.3.   Chapter 17, Section 40 of Medicare Claims Processing Manual
(2/25/2010)

What does this mean for the CDM team or pharmacy CDM team? The CDM team must work to ensure that self-administered drugs for Medicare beneficiaries are properly reported with revenue code 0637, and charges are placed in the noncovered charges field on the claims form. However, for private or other government payers that do include self-administered drugs in the benefit package, CDM teams must ensure not only that these line item charges are properly reported with revenue code 0637 but that the charge is placed in the covered charges field on the claim form or format. Correct capture of the patient's financial class or third party payer at time of admission is required for compliant self-administered drug reporting.

Duplicate Charges on Claim

There are two types of duplicate charges to consider: two line item charges that identify the same service are reported on the claim or coding that does not follow the National Correct Coding Initiative (NCCI) guidelines. Both issues require CDM team consideration.

Coordination of soft coding (coding unit) and hard coding (CDM) is critical. In chapter 4 we discussed the workflow considerations for adding new departments to the CDM. This includes switching coding responsibility from soft coding to hard coding. Failure to effectively communicate the change in coding approach can result in duplicate charges on the claim. When the facility is planning a change from soft coding to hard coding, the CDM team must include a manual review of claims in their conversion process to ensure that claims for the service area do not contain duplicate charges. Although CMS imposes unit limits by utilizing the medically unlikely edits (MUE), duplicate charges could go undetected if the MUE maximum is greater than one. Therefore, it is important for the CDM team to confirm that soft coding has ceased and only hard-coded charges are included on the claim if that is the intent.

Violation of NCCI edits can result in duplicate charges being reported for the same service (Bowman 2008, 120). Column One/Column Two Correct Coding Edit Table and the Mutually Exclusive Coding Edit Table provide a listing of code pairs that should not be reported together unless otherwise warranted and indicated by application of a modifier. When a facility's coding or billing software edits are not properly executed, the result is the facility reporting both charges (duplicate) for the service. NCCI edits are applicable for Medicare. However, many private and other government payers have adopted the NCCI edits. NCCI edits as well as the NCCI Policy Manual for Medicare Services can be downloaded at http://www.cms.hhs.gov/NationalCorrectCodInitEd/. It is important to consider that NCCI edits are updated quarterly, so software edits must be maintained quarterly as well.

How does the CDM fit into following NCCI edits? Let us consider postoperative drug administration. The patient is scheduled for same-day surgery for a knee arthroscopy with meniscectomy (code 29881). In the recovery room, the patient receives multiple IV administrations of fentanyl and dilaudid (96374, 96375, and 96376), which were included on the physician's orders for pain management. After four hours in the recovery room, the patient is discharged to home. A close look at the NCCI edits reveals that the drug administration services (codes 96374, 96375, and 96376) are not reportable with 29881 (*CMS* 2010d). If the facility fails to acknowledge the NCCI edits and reports 96374, 96375, and 96376 on this encounter claim, then the facility is in essence reporting duplicate charges as these services are considered part of the knee arthroscopy surgery that is reported with code 29881.

Off-Campus CDMs

Just as the pharmacy CDM can be a separate CDM, facilities may maintain a separate CDM for off-campus clinics such as wound care clinics or infusion clinics. The CDM team should ensure that the off-campus CDM is current, accurate, and compliant. The CDM team and the off-campus areas should have a close working relationship. Policies and procedures should be in alignment for both areas. Likewise, review and audit responsibilities should be established in advance. Pricing can also be an issue. The CDM team must ensure that off-campus CDMs are included in schedule price reviews.

References

Bowman, S. 2008. *Health Information Management Compliance: Guidelines for Preventing Fraud and Abuse*, 4th ed. Chicago: AHIMA.

Centers for Medicare and Medicaid Services. 2010a. Healthcare Procedure Coding System (HCPCS) Level II.

Centers for Medicare and Medicaid Services. 2010b (rev. Feb. 5). Medicare Claims Processing Manual, Chapter 17, Section 40. http://www.cms.gov/manuals/downloads/clm104c17.pdf.

Centers for Medicare and Medicaid Services. 2010c (rev. Dec. 18). Medicare Benefit Policy Manual, Chapter 15, Section 50.2. http://www.cms.hhs.gov/manuals/Downloads/bp102c15.pdf.

Centers for Medicare and Medicaid Services. 2010d. National Correct Coding Initiative Policy Manual for Medicare Services. NCCI Edits - Hospital Outpatient PPS. http://www.cms.gov/NationalCorrect CodInitEd/NCCIEHOPPS/list.asp#TopOfPage.

Food and Drug Administration. 2010. National Drug Code Directory. http://www.accessdata.fda.gov/scripts/cder/ndc/default.cfm.

Resources

Stone, F., J. Egan, R. LeBoutillier, and D. Blackwelder. 2006 (October). Opening Pandora's box: Pure coding vs. charge master driven coding—a case study at Duke University health system. *Proceedings from AHIMA's 78th National Convention and Exhibit.*

Appendix A

Sample Job Description for the Chargemaster Coordinator

Job Title: CDM (Charge Description Master) Coordinator

Job Summary

Develops, maintains, and reports on the charge description master (CDM); ensures data and charge integrity between the CDM and the hospital departments; researches coding and revenue reporting requirements and uses strategic pricing applications to maximize reimbursement. This position will assure accurate charge design, build, validation, testing, and quality assurance for all changes to the CDM, electronic and paper charge forms, and charge systems applications.

Essential Functions

1. Maintains the CDM by incorporating new charges/services identified by the departments, third-party changes, CMS regulations, federal and state specific coding updates.
2. Performs a detailed, annual review of the CDM that includes identifying CPT and HCPCS Level II codes that have been deleted, added, or replaced; assigning CPT and HCPCS specific codes when appropriate; identifying description changes; and ensuring the nomenclature reflects the procedures performed.
3. Identifies services that are reimbursable but are not being coded; reviews, assigns, and validates revenue codes.
4. Coordinates annual and biannual meetings with department managers, staff and/or physicians regarding new program and procedure developments, equipment acquisitions and validation of inactive codes.
5. Determines charge and charge attributes for new services and products.
6. Communicates CDM changes to the hospital departments and administration, patient accounting, and others who are impacted by the change.

Sources: The University of Utah 1998; Clarian Health Partners n.d. Coordinator-Charge Integrity. http://www.clarian.org/.

7. Maintains audit trail of CDM changes.

8. Distributes correspondence of third-party requirements for coding changes to departments for review of the impending changes.

9. Researches and resolves CPT and HCPCS codes, revenue codes, and other issues referred by the Patient Financial Services department.

10. Uses strategic pricing applications.

11. Uses CMS, third-party payers, and local FI as a technical resource.

12. Establishes and maintains positive working relationships with medical directors, department chairs, and staff.

13. Serves as a resource to hospital departments; for example, assists with the start-up process for new programs and answers implementation questions and regulation questions.

14. Completes and provides management reports as requested.

The preceding essential function statements are not intended to be an exhaustive list of tasks and functions for this position. Other tasks and functions may be assigned as needed to fulfill the mission of the organization.

Qualifications/Knowledge/Skill/Abilities:

- Bachelor's degree in Business Administration or equivalent (required), Master's degree (preferred)
- Five years of experience maintaining price files and record keeping
- Requires knowledge of both clinical and revenue cycle operations
- Requires experience with medical terminology and CPT coding systems
- Requires knowledge of billing and reimbursement processes and methodologies
- Requires computer literacy with experience with Microsoft Office
- Requires excellent written and verbal communication skills with the ability to effectively interact with all levels of internal and external customers
- Requires knowledge regarding CPT-4 and HCPCS coding and UB-92/UB-04 revenue code assignments
- Requires ability to take initiative, effectively use problem-solving skills and adjusts to changes in policy/procedures
- Requires effective organizational skills with attention to detail
- Requires ability to organize and process a high volume of work within established standards
- Requires good interpersonal skills
- Requires ability to work independently
- Requires ability to handle multiple tasks

Appendix B

List of Medicare Revenue Codes

Segment SV2, Element 01 revenue codes for outpatient ancillary services

Pharmacy   **025X**

Pharmacy—General	0250
Pharmacy—Generic Drugs	0251
Pharmacy—Nongeneric Drugs	0252
Pharmacy—Take-Home Drugs	0253
Pharmacy—Drugs Incident to Other Diagnostic Services	0254
Pharmacy—Drugs Incident to Radiology	0255
Pharmacy—Experimental Drugs	0256
Pharmacy—Nonprescription	0257
Pharmacy—IV Solutions	0258
Pharmacy—Other Pharmacy	0259

IV Therapy   **026X**

IV Therapy—General	0260
IV Therapy—Infusion Pump	0261
IV Therapy—IV Therapy/Pharmacy Services	0262
IV Therapy—IV Therapy/Drug/Supply Delivery	0263
IV Therapy—IV Therapy/Supplies	0264
IV Therapy—Other IV Therapy	0269

Medical/Surgical Supplies and Devices   **027X**

Medical/Surgical Supplies and Devices—General	0270
Medical/Surgical Supplies and Devices—Nonsterile Supply	0271
Medical/Surgical Supplies and Devices—Sterile Supply	0272
Medical/Surgical Supplies and Devices—Take-Home Supplies	0273
Medical/Surgical Supplies and Devices—Prosthetic/Orthotic Devices	0274
Medical/Surgical Supplies and Devices—Pacemaker	0275
Medical/Surgical Supplies and Devices—Intraocular Lens	0276

Source: Centers for Medicare and Medicaid Services. 2009b (July 10). Medicare Claims Processing Manual. Chapter 25: Completing and Processing the Form CMS-1450 Data Set. http://www.cms.hhs.gov/manuals/downloads/cim104c25.pdf.

Medical/Surgical Supplies and Devices—Oxygen—Take-Home   0277
Medical/Surgical Supplies and Devices—Other Implants   0278
Medical/Surgical Supplies and Devices—Other Supplies/Devices   0279

Oncology   028X

Oncology—General   0280
Oncology—Other   0289

Durable Medical Equipment (Other than Renal)   029X

DME (Other than Renal)—General   0290
DME (Other than Renal)—Rental   0291
DME (Other than Renal)—Purchase of New DME   0292
DME (Other than Renal)—Purchase of Used DME   0293
DME (Other than Renal)—Supplies/Drugs for DME Effectiveness
    (HHAs Only)   0294
DME (Other than Renal)—Other Equipment   0299

Laboratory   030X

Laboratory—General   0300
Laboratory—Chemistry   0301
Laboratory—Immunology   0302
Laboratory—Renal Patient (Home)   0303
Laboratory—Nonroutine Dialysis   0304
Laboratory—Hematology   0305
Laboratory—Bacteriology and Microbiology   0306
Laboratory—Urology   0307
Laboratory—Other Laboratory   0309

Laboratory Pathological   031X

Laboratory Pathological—General   0310
Laboratory Pathological—Cytology   0311
Laboratory Pathological—Histology   0312
Laboratory Pathological—Biopsy   0314
Laboratory Pathological—Other   0319

Radiology—Diagnostic   032X

Radiology—Diagnostic—General   0320
Radiology—Diagnostic—Angiocardiography 0321
Radiology—Diagnostic—Arthrography   0322
Radiology—Diagnostic—Arteriography   0323
Radiology—Diagnostic—Chest X-ray   0324
Radiology—Diagnostic—Other   0329

Radiology—Therapeutic   **033X**

    Radiology—Therapeutic—General   0330
    Radiology—Therapeutic—Chemotherapy—Injected   0331
    Radiology—Therapeutic—Chemotherapy—Oral   0332
    Radiology—Therapeutic—Radiation Therapy   0333
    Radiology—Therapeutic—Chemotherapy—IV   0335
    Radiology—Therapeutic—Other   0339

Nuclear Medicine   **034X**

    Nuclear Medicine—General   0340
    Nuclear Medicine—Diagnostic   0341
    Nuclear Medicine—Therapeutic   0342
    Nuclear Medicine—Diagnostic Radiopharmaceuticals   0343
    Nuclear Medicine—Therapeutic Radiopharmaceuticals   0344
    Nuclear Medicine—Other   0349

CT Scan   **035X**

    CT Scan—General   0350
    CT Scan—Head Scan   0351
    CT Scan—Body Scan   0352
    CT Scan—Other CT Scans   0359

Operating Room Services   036X

    Operating Room Services—General   0360
    Operating Room Services—Minor Surgery   0361
    Operating Room Services—Organ Transplant—Other than Kidney   0362
    Operating Room Services—Kidney Transplant   0367
    Operating Room Services—Other Operating Room Services   0369

Anesthesia   **037X**

    Anesthesia—General   0370
    Anesthesia—Anesthesia Incident to Radiology   0371
    Anesthesia—Anesthesia Incident to Other Diagnostic Services   0372
    Anesthesia—Acupuncture   0374
    Anesthesia—Other Anesthesia   0379

Blood   **038X**

    Blood—General   0380
    Blood—Packed Red Cells   0381
    Blood—Whole Blood   0382
    Blood—Plasma   0383
    Blood—Platelets   0384
    Blood—Leukocytes   0385

Speech-Language Pathology—Group Rate   0443
Speech-Language Pathology—Evaluation or Reevaluation   0444
Speech-Language Pathology—Other Speech-Language Pathology   0449

Emergency Room   **045X**

Emergency Room—General   0450
Emergency Room—EMTALA Emergency Medical Screening Services   0451
Emergency Room—ER Beyond EMTALA Screening   0452
Emergency Room—Urgent Care   0456
Emergency Room—Other Emergency Room   0459

Pulmonary Function   **046X**

Pulmonary Function—General   0460
Pulmonary Function—Other Pulmonary Function   0469

Audiology   **047X**

Audiology—General   0470
Audiology—Diagnostic   0471
Audiology—Treatment   0472
Audiology—Other Audiology   0479

Cardiology   **048X**

Cardiology—General   0480
Cardiology—Cardiac Cath Lab   0481
Cardiology—Stress Test   0482
Cardiology—Echocardiology   0483
Cardiology—Other Cardiology   0489

Ambulatory Surgical Care   **049X**

Ambulatory Surgical Care—General   0490
Ambulatory Surgical Care—Other Ambulatory Surgical Care   0499

Outpatient Services   **050X**

Outpatient Services—General   0500
Outpatient Services—Other Outpatient Services   0509

Clinic   **051X**

Clinic—General   0510
Clinic—Chronic Pain Center   0511
Clinic—Dental Clinic   0512
Clinic—Psychiatric Clinic   0513
Clinic—OB/GYN Clinic   0514
Clinic—Pediatric Clinic   0515
Clinic—Urgent Care Clinic   0516

| Clinic—Family Practice Clinic | 0517 |
| Clinic—Other Clinic | 0519 |

Freestanding Clinic   **052X**

Freestanding Clinic—General	0520
Freestanding Clinic—Clinic visit by member to RHC/FQHC	0521
Freestanding Clinic—Home visit by RHC/FQHC practitioner	0522
Freestanding Clinic—Family Practice Clinic	0523
Freestanding Clinic—Visit by RHC/FQHC Practitioner to a Member in a Covered Part A Stay at SNF	0524
Freestanding Clinic—Visit by RHC/FQHC Practitioner to a member in an SNF (Not in a Covered Part A stay) or NF or ICF MR or Other Residential Facility	0525
Freestanding Clinic—Urgent Care Clinic	0526
Freestanding Clinic—Visiting Nurse Service to a Member's Home in a Home Health Shortage Area	0527
Freestanding Clinic—Visit by RHC/FQHC Practitioner to other non-RHC/FQHC site (e.g. Scene of Accident)	0528
Freestanding Clinic—Other Freestanding Clinic	0529

Osteopathic Services   **053X**

Osteopathic Services—General	0530
Osteopathic Services—Osteopathic Therapy	0531
Osteopathic Services—Other Osteopathic Services	0539

Ambulance   **054X**

Ambulance—General	0540
Ambulance—Supplies	0541
Ambulance—Medical Transport	0542
Ambulance—Heart Mobile	0543
Ambulance—Oxygen	0544
Ambulance—Air Ambulance	0545
Ambulance—Neonatal Ambulance Services	0546
Ambulance—Pharmacy	0547
Ambulance—Telephone Transmission EKG	0548
Ambulance—Other Ambulance	0549

Magnetic Resonance Technology (MRT)   **061X**

Magnetic Resonance Imaging—General	0610
Magnetic Resonance Imaging—Brain (Including Brain Stem)	0611
Magnetic Resonance Imaging—Spinal Cord (Including Spine)	0612
Reserved	0613
Magnetic Resonance Imaging—Other MRI	0614

Magnetic Resonance Angiography—Head and Neck	0615
Magnetic Resonance Angiography—Lower Extremities	0616
Reserved	0617
Magnetic Resonance Angiography—Other MRA	0618
Magnetic Resonance Technology—Other MRT	0619

Medical/Surgical Supplies—Extension of 027X   **062X**

Medical/Surgical Supplies (Extension of 027X)—Supplies Incident to Radiology	0621
Medical/Surgical Supplies (Extension of 027X)—Supplies Incident to Other Diagnostic Services	0622
Medical/Surgical Supplies (Extension of 027X)—Surgical Dressings	0623
Medical/Surgical Supplies (Extension of 027X)—FDA Investigational Devices	0624

Pharmacy—Extension of 025X   **063X**

Reserved	0630
Pharmacy- (Extension of 025X)—Single Source Drug	0631
Pharmacy- (Extension of 025X)—Multiple Source Drug	0632
Pharmacy- (Extension of 025X)—Restrictive Prescription	0633
Pharmacy- (Extension of 025X)—Erythropoietin (EPO) Less than 10,000 Units	0634
Pharmacy- (Extension of 025X)—Erythropoietin (EPO) 10,000 or More Units	0635
Pharmacy- (Extension of 025X)—Drugs Requiring Detailed Coding	0636
Pharmacy- (Extension of 025X)—Self-Administrable Drugs	0637

Trauma Response   **068X**

Not Used	0680
Trauma Response—Level I	0681
Trauma Response—Level II	0682
Trauma Response—Level III	0683
Trauma Response—Level IV	0684
Other trauma response	0689

Cast Room   **070X**

Cast Room—General	0700
Cast Room—Other Cast Room	0709

Recovery Room   **071X**

Recovery Room—General	0710
Recovery Room—Other Recovery Room	0719

EKG/ECG (Electrocardiogram)   **073X**

    EKG/ECG (Electrocardiogram)—General   0730
    EKG/ECG (Electrocardiogram)—Holter Monitor   0731
    EKG/ECG (Electrocardiogram)—Telemetry   0732
    EKG/ECG (Electrocardiogram)—Other EKG/ECG   0739

EEG (Electroencephalogram)   **074X**

    EEG (Electroencephalogram)—General   0740
    EEG (Electroencephalogram)—Other EEG   0749

Gastrointestinal Services   **075X**

    Gastrointestinal Services—General   0750
    Gastrointestinal Services—Other Gastrointestinal   0759

Treatment or Observation Room   **076X**

    Treatment or Observation Room—General   0760
    Treatment or Observation Room—Treatment Room   0761
    Treatment or Observation Room—Observation Hours   0762
    Treatment or Observation Room—Other Specialty Services 0769

Preventive Care Services   **077X**

    Preventive Care Services—General   0770
    Preventive Care Services—Vaccine Administration   0771
    Reserved   0779

Extracorporeal Shock Wave Therapy (formerly Lithotripsy)   **079X**

    Extracorporeal Shock Wave Therapy (formerly Lithotripsy)—General   0790
    Reserved   0799

Organ Acquisition   **081X**

    Organ Acquisition—General   0810
    Organ Acquisition—Living Donor   0811
    Organ Acquisition—Cadaver Donor   0812
    Organ Acquisition—Unknown Donor   0813
    Organ Acquisition—Unsuccessful Organ Search—Donor Bank Charges   0814
    Organ Acquisition—Other Donor   0819

Hemodialysis—Outpatient or Home   **082X**

    Hemodialysis—Outpatient or Home Dialysis—General   0820
    Hemodialysis—Outpatient or Home Dialysis—Hemodialysis/Composite
      or Other Rate   0821
    Hemodialysis—Outpatient or Home Dialysis—Home Supplies 0822
    Hemodialysis—Outpatient or Home Dialysis—Home Equipment 0823

Hemodialysis—Outpatient or Home Dialysis—Maintenance/100%	0824
Hemodialysis—Outpatient or Home Dialysis—Support Services	0825
Hemodialysis—Outpatient or Home Dialysis—Other Outpatient Hemodialysis	0829

Peritoneal Dialysis—Outpatient or Home   083X

Peritoneal Dialysis—Outpatient or Home—General	0830
Peritoneal Dialysis—Outpatient or Home—Peritoneal/Composite or Other Rate	0831
Peritoneal Dialysis—Outpatient or Home—Home Supplies	0832
Peritoneal Dialysis—Outpatient or Home—Home Equipment	0833
Peritoneal Dialysis—Outpatient or Home—Maintenance/100%	0834
Peritoneal Dialysis—Outpatient or Home—Support Services	0835
Peritoneal Dialysis—Outpatient or Home—Other Peritoneal Dialysis	0839

CAPD (Dialysis)—Outpatient or Home   084X

CAPD (Dialysis)—Outpatient or Home—General	0840
CAPD (Dialysis)—Outpatient or Home—CAPD/Composite or Other Rate	0841
CAPD (Dialysis)—Outpatient or Home—Home Supplies	0842
CAPD (Dialysis)—Outpatient or Home—Home Equipment	0843
CAPD (Dialysis)—Outpatient or Home—Maintenance/100%	0844
CAPD (Dialysis)—Outpatient or Home—Support Services	0845
CAPD (Dialysis)—Outpatient or Home—OtherCAPD Dialysis	0849

CCPD (Dialysis)—Outpatient or Home   085X

CCPD (Dialysis)—Outpatient or Home—General	0850
CCPD (Dialysis)—Outpatient or Home—CCPD/Composite or Other Rate	0851
CCPD (Dialysis)—Outpatient or Home—Home Supplies	0852
CCPD (Dialysis)—Outpatient or Home—Home Equipment	0853
CCPD (Dialysis)—Outpatient or Home—Maintenance/100%	0854
CCPD (Dialysis)—Outpatient or Home—Support Services	0855
CCPD (Dialysis)—Outpatient or Home—Other CCPD Dialysis	0859

Reserved for Dialysis (National Assignment)   086X

Reserved for Dialysis (National Assignment)   087X

Miscellaneous Dialysis   088X

Miscellaneous Dialysis—General	0880
Miscellaneous Dialysis—Ultrafiltration	0881
Miscellaneous Dialysis—Home Dialysis Aid Visit	0882
Miscellaneous Dialysis—Other Miscellaneous Dialysis	0889

Reserved for National Assignment   **089X**

Behavioral Health Treatments/Services (also see 091X, an extension
of 090X)   **090X**

Behavioral Health Treatments/Services
(also see 091X, an extension of 090X)—General   0900
Behavioral Health Treatments/Services
(also see 091X, an extension of 090X)—Electroshock Treatment   0901
Behavioral Health Treatments/Services
(also see 091X, an extension of 090X)—Milieu Therapy   0902
Behavioral Health Treatments/Services
(also see 091X, an extension of 090X)—Play Therapy   0903
Behavioral Health Treatments/Services
(also see 091X, an extension of 090X)—Activity Therapy   0904
Behavioral Health Treatments/Services (also see 091X,
an extension of 090X)—Intensive Outpatient Services—Psychiatric   0905
Behavioral Health Treatments/Services (also see 091X,
an extension of 090X)—Intensive Outpatient Services—
Chemical Dependency   0906
Behavioral Health Treatments/Services (also see 091X,
an extension of 090X)—Community Behavioral Health
Program (Day Treatment)   0907
Behavioral Health Treatments/Services (also see 091X,
an extension of 090X)—Reserved for National Use   0908
Behavioral Health Treatments/Services (also see 091X, an extension
of 090X)—Reserved for National Use   0909

Behavioral Health Treatments/Services—Extension of 090X   **091X**

Behavioral Health Treatments/Services—Extension of 090X—
Reserved for National Use   0910
Behavioral Health Treatments/Services—Extension of 090X—
Rehabilitation   0911
Behavioral Health Treatments/Services—Extension of 090X—
Partial Hospitalization—Less Intensive   0912
Behavioral Health Treatments/Services—Extension of 090X—
Partial Hospitalization—Intensive   0913
Behavioral Health Treatments/Services—Extension of 090X—
Individual Therapy   0914
Behavioral Health Treatments/Services—Extension of 090X—
Group Therapy   0915
Behavioral Health Treatments/Services—Extension of 090X—
Family Therapy   0916

Behavioral Health Treatments/Services—Extension of 090X—
  Biofeedback   0917
Behavioral Health Treatments/Services—Extension of 090X—
  Testing   0918
Behavioral Health Treatments/Services—Extension of 090X—
  Other Behavioral Health Treatments/Services   0919

Other Diagnostic Services   **092X**

  Other Diagnostic Services—General   0920
  Other Diagnostic Services—Peripheral Vascular Lab   0921
  Other Diagnostic Services—Electromyelogram   0922
  Other Diagnostic Services—Pap Smear   0923
  Other Diagnostic Services—Allergy Test   0924
  Other Diagnostic Services—Pregnancy Test   0925
  Other Diagnostic Services—Other Diagnostic Service   0929

Medical Rehabilitation Day Program   **093X**

  Medical Rehabilitation Day Program—Half Day   0931
  Medical Rehabilitation Day Program—Full Day   0932

Other Therapeutic Services (also see 095X, extension of 094X)   **094X**

  Other Therapeutic Services—General   0940
  Other Therapeutic Services—Recreational Therapy   0941
  Other Therapeutic Services—Education/Training   0942
  Other Therapeutic Services—Cardiac Rehabilitation   0943
  Other Therapeutic Services—Drug Rehabilitation   0944
  Other Therapeutic Services—Alcohol Rehabilitation   0945
  Other Therapeutic Services—Complex Medical Equipment—Routine   0946
  Other Therapeutic Services—Complex Medical Equipment—Ancillary   0947
  Other Therapeutic Services—Other Therapeutic Services   0949

Other Therapeutic Services (extension of 094X)   **095X**

  Reserved   0950
  Other Therapeutic Services—Athletic Training   0951
  Other Therapeutic Services—Kinesiotherapy   0952

Professional Fees   **096X**

  Professional Fees—General   0960
  Professional Fees—Psychiatric   0961
  Professional Fees—Ophthalmology   0962
  Professional Fees—Anesthesiologist (MD)   0963
  Professional Fees—Anesthetist (CRNA)   0964

Professional Fees—Other Professional Fees   0969

Professional Fees (extension of 096X)   **097X**

    Professional Fees—Laboratory   0971
    Professional Fees—Radiology—Diagnostic   0972
    Professional Fees—Radiology—Therapeutic   0973
    Professional Fees—Radiology—Nuclear Medicine   0974
    Professional Fees—Operating Room   0975
    Professional Fees—Respiratory Therapy   0976
    Professional Fees—Physical Therapy   0977
    Professional Fees—Occupational Therapy   0978
    Professional Fees—Speech Pathology   0979

Professional Fees (extension of 096X and 097X)   **098X**

    Professional Fees—Emergency Room   0981
    Professional Fees—Outpatient Services   0982
    Professional Fees—Clinic   0983
    Professional Fees—Medical Social Services   0984
    Professional Fees—EKG   0985
    Professional Fees—EEG   0986
    Professional Fccs—Hospital Visit   0987
    Professional Fees—Consultation   0988
    Professional Fees—Private-Duty Nurse   0989

Patient Convenience Items   **099X**

    Patient Convenience Items—General   0990
    Patient Convenience Items—Cafeteria/Guest Tray   0991
    Patient Convenience Items—Private Linen Service   0992
    Patient Convenience Items—Telephone/Telegraph   0993
    Patient Convenience Items—TV/Radio   0994
    Patient Convenience Items—Nonpatient Room Rentals 0995
    Patient Convenience Items—Late Discharge Charge   0996
    Patient Convenience Items—Admission Kits   0997
    Patient Convenience Items—Beauty Shop/Barber   0998
    Patient Convenience Items—Other Patient Convenience Items 0999

Alternative Therapy Services   **210X**

Appendix C

Practice Brief: The Care and Maintenance of Chargemasters (Updated)

Editor's note: This update replaces the July/August 1999 practice brief "The Care and Maintenance of Charge Masters."

The various supplies and services listed on the Chargemaster for the average facility drives reimbursement for the vast majority of items listed on UB-04 claims. The Chargemaster—also called the charge description master (CDM)—is simply a master price list of supplies, devices, medications, services, procedures, and other items for which a distinct charge to the patient exists. It is a financial management form that contains information about the organization's charges for the healthcare services it provides to patients. The CDM collects information on all the goods and services the organization provides to its patients. Therefore, the responsibility for maintaining the database may fall to several individual departments (e.g., laboratory radiology). In addition, some organizations choose to have a central CDM position that interacts with the various departments to ensure that accurate data are maintained in the CDM and address any issues that may arise.

On every front, healthcare is advancing by leaps and bounds. At the same time, organizations and providers struggle to receive appropriate reimbursement for the care they provide. In the midst of MS-DRGs, severity-adjusted DRGs, and annual code updates to both the ICD-9-CM classification and CPT nomenclature systems, the struggle is an ongoing issue for many organizations. As profit margins narrow and the cost of training staff and implementing new reimbursement mechanisms grow, senior management must determine where best to focus limited resources to ensure that the revenue cycle is healthy.

A current and accurate Chargemaster is vital to any healthcare provider seeking proper reimbursement and a key indicator in a healthy revenue cycle. The CDM allows the organization to capture charges as they occur, almost in real time. Without a healthy CDM process, the facility would not receive proper reimbursement, and incoming revenue could potentially come to a halt. Among the negative effects that may result from an inaccurate Chargemaster are:

- Overpayment or overcharging
- Underpayment or undercharging

- Claims rejections
- Fines
- Penalties

Because a Chargemaster is an automated process that results in billing numerous services for high volumes of patients—often without human intervention—there is a high risk that a single coding or mapping error could spawn error after error before it is identified and corrected. For example, if the Chargemaster is incorrectly developed with a chest x-ray mapped to a unit of service of 10 instead of 1, as the x-ray technician charges for the CPT code associated with a chest x-ray, the patient would be charged for 10 x-rays. In addition, the CDM usually drives more than 70 percent of an organization's revenue cycle dollars because it focuses on outpatient services and supplies. Although these services and supplies may be low in dollar value, they are very often high in terms of volume. As a result, outpatient services can include up to 25,000 line items within the CDM.

Key Elements of a Chargemaster List

The content and layout of a healthcare provider's Chargemaster may vary from one organization to the next. However, one can expect to see the following data elements in the typical Chargemaster file:

- Charge description: Also known as "item description" and other names, this title describes the supply, device, medication, service, procedure, or other item provided or performed. There is no set format or vocabulary for this description, but facilities are typically bound by space constraints to only a limited number of characters to describe each item. Each description should be unique to a facility. Furthermore, each description should be separately identifiable. For example, no two line items should have the exact same description. Keep in mind that the charge description will appear on the patient's detailed bill. Not only do staff members posting charges need to be able to correctly identify which charges to post on a patient's account but patients also should have some understanding of what the charge represents on the detailed bill. When linked to a CPT or HCPCS code, the charge description should match the CPT or HCPCS code descriptor as closely as possible.
- CPT or HCPCS code: The corresponding CPT or HCPCS level II code that identifies the specific service or procedure. Modifiers may or may not be included, depending on the circumstances. However, not all services and procedures listed on the Chargemaster have a corresponding code. Since all supplies and services may not require a code assignment and the use of unlisted or nonspecific codes is not desirable to the organization, it may be better to leave this field blank in these instances.

- Revenue code: A four-digit code number representing a specific accommodation, ancillary service, or billing calculation required for Medicare billing. The National Uniform Billing Committee and Centers for Medicare and Medicaid Services (CMS) update the list of acceptable revenue codes on an ongoing basis.
- Charge: The charge dollar amount represents the amount charged for the item and the amount that will appear on the patient's detailed bill. Some facilities prefer to use the term "price" instead of "charge."
- Department code: The department code or general ledger number, generally two or three digits, is used for accounting purposes to distribute the revenue to the appropriate department.
- Charge code: An internally assigned unique number that identifies each specific item listed on the Chargemaster. This is also referred to as a "charge description number," "item code," or "CDM number."
- Charge status: The charge status or activity date element indicates the most recent activity of an item. This allows a facility to monitor whether a line item has been charged to any patient's bill in a period of time.

CDM example:

Charge Description	CPT/ HCPCS Code	Revenue Code	Charge	Department Code	Charge Code	Charge status
Nasal bone x-ray	70160	320	150.00	15	2214111000	12/1/2001
Thyroid Sonogram	76536	320	250.00	15	2110410000	1/1/2003
Echo Encephalogram	76506	320	1,500.00	15	2326222111	7/1/2005

The Chargemaster Committee

Ideally, Chargemaster maintenance should not be the exclusive responsibility of one individual. Rather, a committee composed of key facility representatives should share this responsibility jointly. This format will contribute to the accuracy and quality of both the document database and Chargemaster review process. For example, the HIM department understands clinical procedure codes, the pharmacy department understands the medications and dosages and their respective codes, and the finance department understands the charge formulas. Proper Chargemaster maintenance requires expertise in coding, billing regulations, clinical procedures, and health record documentation. The entire CDM should be reviewed periodically, but at a minimum it should be reviewed annually to coincide with annual code updates and organizational changes. Identification and substantiation of the actual costs of providing healthcare services is an integral part of the CDM update and should also be considered when updating the CDM. For most organizations the finance department assumes responsibility for the annual update to the CDM.

The Chargemaster committee should include representation from:

- HIM
- Financial services or the business office
- Information systems
- Corporate compliance
- Department management from various service areas that generate charges including:
  - Radiology
  - Laboratory
  - Respiratory therapy
  - Cardiac catheterization laboratory
  - Physical therapy
  - Emergency department
  - Nursing
- Physicians, as needed

Responsibilities of the Chargemaster committee include:

- Developing policies and procedures for the Chargemaster review process
- Performing Chargemaster review at least annually when new CPT and HCPCS codes are available
- Attending to key elements of the annual Chargemaster review, including:
  - Reviewing all CPT and HCPCS codes for accuracy, validity, and relationship to charge description number
  - Reviewing all charge descriptions for accuracy and clinical appropriateness
  - Reviewing all revenue codes for accuracy and linkage to charge description numbers
  - Ensuring that the usage of all CPT, HCPCS, and revenue codes are in compliance with Medicare guidelines or other existing payer contracts
  - Reviewing all charge dollar amounts for appropriateness by payer
  - Reviewing all charge codes for uniqueness and validity
  - Reviewing all department code numbers for uniqueness and validity
- Performing ongoing Chargemaster maintenance as the facility adds or deletes new procedures, updates technology, or changes services provided
- Ensuring that all necessary maintenance to systems affected by changes to the Chargemaster (such as order entry feeder systems, charge tickets, and interfaces) is performed when Chargemaster maintenance is performed

- Performing tests to make sure that changes to the Chargemaster result in the desired outcome
- Educating all clinical department directors on the Chargemaster and the effect of the Chargemaster on corporate compliance
- Establishing a procedure to allow clinical department directors to submit Chargemaster change requests for new, deleted, or revised procedures or services
- Ensuring there is no duplication of code assignment by coders and Chargemaster-assigned codes in any department (e.g., interventional radiology or cardiology catheterization laboratory)
- Reviewing all charge ticket and order entry screens for accuracy against the Chargemaster and appropriate mapping to CPT or HCPCS codes when required
- Reviewing and complying with directives in Medicare transmittals, Medicare manual updates, and official coding guidelines
- Complying with guidelines in the National Correct Coding Initiative, Outpatient Code Editor edits, and any other coding or bundling edits
- Considering carefully any application that involves one charge description number that expands into more than one CPT or HCPCS code to prevent inadvertent unbundling and unearned reimbursement for services
- Reviewing and taking action on all remittance advice denials involving HCPCS or CPT coding rules and guidelines or CMS payer rules
- Educating all staff affected by changes to the Chargemaster in a timely fashion

References

Abdelhak, M. 1996. *Health Information: Management of a Strategic Resource.* Philadelphia: W.B. Saunders Company.

Bowman, S. 2007. *Health Information Management Compliance: Guidelines for Preventing Fraud and Abuse,* 4th ed. Chicago: AHIMA.

CPT codes and resources published by the American Medical Association: www.ama-assn.org/ama/pub/physician-resources/solutions-managing-your-practice/coding-billing-insurance/cpt.shtml.

Expert Advice on Preparing for the APCs. 1999. *Medical Record Briefing* 14(4)3.

Dietz, M. S. 2005 (October). Ensure equitable reimbursement through an accurate charge description master. AHIMA's 77th National Convention and Exhibit Proceedings. Available online in the AHIMA Body of Knowledge at www.ahima.org.

Drach, M., A. Davis, and C. Sagrati. 2001 (January). Ten steps to successful chargemaster reviews. *Journal of AHIMA* 72(1):42–48.

Falconer, C. 1994. *St. Anthony's UB-92 Editor: A Guide to Medicare Billing.* Reston, VA: St. Anthony Publishing.

HCPCS codes and resources: http://www.cms.gov/MedHCPCSGenInfo/.

Meeter, C. 2008. Chargemaster nuts and bolts. Northern California Healthcare Financial Management Association Conference in Spring 2008. Available online at www.hfma-nca.org/documents/2008%20Spring%20Conference%20presentations/Revenue%20Cycle/PP%20Chargemaster%20Nuts%20and%20Bolts%2002%2013%2008_Cathy%20Meeter.pdf.

National Correct Coding Initiative, National Technical Information Service Web site: www.ntis.gov/products/cci.aspx.

National Correct Coding Initiative, CMS Web site: http://www.cms.gov/NationalCorrectCodInitEd/.

Outpatient Code Editor: http://www.cms.gov/OutpatientCodeEdit/Revenue codes can be found in chapter 25, section 75.4, of the Medicare Claims Processing Manual: http://www.cms.gov/manuals/downloads/clm104c25.pdf.

Richard, T. 1999. *The Hospital Chargemaster Guide.* Reston, VA: St. Anthony Publishing.

Richey, J. 2001 (January). A new approach to chargemaster management." *Journal of AHIMA* 72(1):51–55.

Schraffenberger, L. A., and Kuehn. 2007. *Effective Management of Coding Services.* Chicago AHIMA.

Stone, F., J. Egan, R. LeBoutillier, and D. Blackwelder. 2006 (October). Opening pandora's box: Pure coding vs. charge master driven coding—A case study at Duke University health system. AHIMA's 78th National Convention and Exhibit Proceedings. Available online in the AHIMA Body of Knowledge at www.ahima.org.

Prepared by

Judy A. Bielby, MBA, RHIA, CPHQ, CCS

Prepared by (original)

Harry Rhodes, MBA, RHIA, HIM practice manager

Acknowledgments (original)

Rita Scichilone, MHSA, RHIA, CCS, CCS-P
Dianne Willard, MBA, RHIA, CCS-P

Index